CONCILIUM

Religion in the Eighties

CONCILIUM

Concilium 153 (3/1982): Dogma

JESUS, SON OF GOD?

Edited by

Edward Schillebeeckx

and

Johannes-Baptist Metz

English Language Editor
Marcus Lefébure

T. & T. CLARK LTD.
Edinburgh

THE SEABURY PRESS
New York

March 1982
T. & T. Clark Ltd., 36 George Street, Edinburgh EH2 2LQ
ISBN: 0 567 30033 1

The Seabury Press, 815 Second Avenue, New York, NY 10017
ISBN: 0 8164 2384 9

Library of Congress Catalog Card No.: 81-85840

Printed in Scotland by William Blackwood & Sons Ltd., Edinburgh

Concilium: Monthly except July and August
Subscriptions 1982: UK and Rest of the World £27·00, postage and handling included;
USA and Canada, all applications for subscriptions and enquiries about *Concilium*
should be addressed to The Seabury Press, 815 Second Avenue, New York, NY 10017,
USA.

CONTENTS

Part III
What sense can the use of the term 'Son of God' have in Non-Christian cultures, such as that of Asia?

Part IV
Towards a Synthesis: A Reflection on the Issue as a Whole

Editorial: Jesus as Son of God

BELIEF IN Jesus of Nazareth as the Son of God lies at the root not only of the New Testament but also of the whole of the way in which Christianity has been lived throughout the ages. This issue of *Concilium* concentrates entirely on this dogmatic problem.

For many Christians this Jesus has become a kind of alien divinity, prised out of the concrete history of salvation. The result obviously is that he is seen as having no creative influence on life as we experience it. Christological dogma often developed an a-political or even anti-political posture, and this obviously resulted in Christians being accused of being a-dogmatic or anti-dogmatic if and when they were politically committed (Wiederkehr). The result was predictable: the cohesion between dogmatic belief and practical behaviour has been frequently torn apart.

During the last twenty years there has been a sharp reaction to all this. It emanated from various corners and showed a variety of approaches. It sprang up from the cultural and social experiences of the faithful today, from theologians who caught up with the problem, as well as from basic communities and departments of theology. Moreover, the inevitable encounter of Christianity with other world religions has had a profound influence on the religious scenario in the West. To illustrate this one has to realise that in France Islam is now the second religion after Catholicism. These encounters with other world religions are bound to affect Christians' own understanding of Jesus Christ.

Moreover, many of the faithful have developed a greater political awareness with the result that they have taken a fresh look at the way the basic confession of faith should find practical expression in life as it is today. This is why in his earthly, human condition, his prophetic words and deeds, and finally in his death as a prophet and martyr, Jesus has become far more important to many in their practical situation than was the case during the last centuries.

The identity of the earthly Jesus with the post-paschal Christ in heaven is a basic hermeneutical principle. Here there is obviously room for stressing one aspect or another, and such emphases are perfectly legitimate. Moreover, every age produces its own. Yet, with all this variety of interpretation it is the duty of the theologian to examine critically whether the mystery of salvation, which is Jesus, does not get distorted at the expense of a basic Christian conformity to the demands of God's kingdom as Jesus demonstrated their fulfilment in his conduct and his person. This means that we must avoid false dilemma between a 'Jesuology' (meaning: a Jesus detached from Christ or the Son of God) and a 'Christology' (meaning here, a Christ without Jesus).

The crucial point here is the basic Christian conviction that *the man Jesus himself* is Son of God. In the concluding article of this issue K. Rahner rightly observes that all Christians have to pass through the Chalcedon phase, but that this phase is transitional and, in the end, not final: the truth aimed at and glimpsed at always exceeds the limits of human concepts and even more so their verbalisation. As in the past, modern attempts to make the mystery of Jesus more accessible to human belief cannot rise above the level of experimentation. There is no way of finding an adequate formula to express what is beyond words.

In the first part of this issue the attempt is made to analyse what the main emphases are in the practice and theology of the confession of Jesus as the Son of God (B. McDermott). Two dimensions are extremely important here if we want to judge contemporary Christologies in a way that is justified and convincing. First of all, there is the fact of the metaphorical and 'analogous' way in which we speak about religious belief: 'Jesus is the Son of God' (Nicholas Lash). Secondly there is the fact that in the New Testament the Christological themes are dealt with in the context of salvation and ensconced in a practical soteriological context (D. Wiederkehr and Jon Sobrino).

The second part examines in detail the use of the expression 'son of God' in both the Old and the New Testaments. H. Haag tackles it in the Old Testament, and where he leaves off, B. van Iersel takes over to deal with it as it appears in the New Testament. From this it appears that there is a close connection between the New Testament use of the term 'son of God' and the way it is rooted in the Old Testament. On the other hand, the idea that the first generation of Christians simply applied the messianic title of 'son of God' to Jesus is not really tenable. In Jesus the title of 'son of God' is charged with the actual and personal life-story of Jesus of Nazareth.

This is followed by Geoffrey Wainwright who examines the pros and cons of praying directly to Jesus instead of 'to the Father *through* the Son'. And he refers *en passant* to the dogmatic implications of liturgical prayer.

The approach of Chalcedon to the confession of Jesus as the Son of God was different from that of the New Testament in that it was wholly static. This was very different from that of the New Testament, and the whole soteriological and practical potential of this confession vanished into the background, particularly in the way it affected traditional thinking and practice. So an examination of the formula of Chalcedon became imperative. This investigation concentrates on what the Council wanted to establish once and for all, and on the way this was actually brought about, particularly on how the Chalcedon model was historically conditioned (T. van Bavel).

Cultural and religious exchanges between the continents gave rise to new challenges in the area of Christology. This affected not only the western versions of Christology but also the African and eastern interpretations of belief in Jesus as the Son of God. In spite of the fact that missiological scholars have been concerned with this problem for years, the demand for indigenisation and acculturation has not yielded much progress. Indeed, it is not simply a matter of 'translation' concerned simply with stripping the data of revelation off its western cultural history and replacing it by giving it a non-western appearance. This kind of approach remains non-dialectic and positivistic where culture is understood as a complex whole.

The adaptative approach is no more satisfactory when it simply tries to substitute African Bantu philosophy for that of Thomas Aquinas. This approach always proceeded from western preconceptions and for that reason has found little response in African culture.To attempt to solve the problem of 'Christology' and 'culture' by appealing directly to the Bible while by-passing the whole Christian tradition is no solution either. This overlooks the fact that, whatever its religious significance, the Bible is and remains itself also a cultural document. To try to graft the Church of the New Testament on to African or Asiatic cultures only leads to cheap solutions which hope that the real problem will go away. No theology can ignore the cultural issue because theology itself is also a cultural process. And so theologians have recently begun to look for a solution in what is called contextual methodology.[1]

This approach starts from people's need of some *cultural identity* which remains stable underneath all kinds of cultural changes. A model of such a methodology requires a deeper reflection on how tradition comes about. This demands a critical approach towards both local traditions and the existing western Christian tradition, as well as abandoning a paternalistic, neo-colonialist attitude. In any case, it is difficult to maintain that the African and Asiatic Christologies have to pass through the twenty-centuries-old history of the western churches before they can be seriously considered as sister-communities on an equal level. Every single Christology is embedded in a 'context' and therefore no Christology can claim any kind of superiority merely on the basis of its particular inculturation. The gospel of Jesus the Son of God who heralded and brought eschatological salvation to all mankind, is 'transcultural' in essence even though always expressed in a given cultural context in the beginning, here and now, and in the centuries to come. Only when incarnated in a concrete cultural context and therefore sharing in the limitations of culture can the gospel become a living reality. And this applies also to Christology. Whenever the Christian gospel comes to life in a definite particular cultural context, it can be the revelation of God's universality.

This whole area is still riddled with problems for which no solution has been found as yet. It would seem that, given the many cross-cultural contacts today and the growing presence of Islam and the eastern religions in the West, this problem will become one of the most urgent for any emerging Christology which wants to be true to the gospel as well as culturally meaningful in practice, both now and in the near future. This growing practical problem could not be fully dealt with in this one issue. So A. Pieris, Director of the Buddhist-Christian 'Centre for research and encounter' in Kelaniya (Sri Lanka), was asked what the expression 'Son of God' could mean for people belonging to an Asiatic, non-Christian religious culture. In a kind of paradigmatic way his article shows both the difficulties and the liberating potential of a Christology rooted in a cultural context which, like the New Testament, preserves a soteriological practical foundation.

Finally, the two editors of this dogmatic issue approached Karl Rahner, an elder theological colleague still very much alive to the problems of his profession, to contribute a concluding article. This was not meant to be a paternalistic final assessment of this issue (something he himself would repudiate). We rather wanted him to speak from his own long theological experience and reflection in order to give some intellectually acceptable and accessible encouragement to those Christians (whether theologically qualified or not) who, informed by the gospel and the great Christological councils, are courageous and loyal enough to put our way of confessing Jesus as Son of God in a way which, because of the historical and cultural context, was not possible in the context of the first centuries of Christianity.

E. SCHILLEBEECKX
J.-B. METZ

Translated by T. L. Westow

Note

1. See *inter alia*: Shoki Coe 'In search of renewal in theological education' *Theological Education* 9 (1973) 233-243; Rob Schreiter 'Issues facing contextual theology today' *Verbum* 14 (1980) 267-278; Louis J. Luzbetak 'Signs of progress in contextual methodology' *Verbum* 22 (1981) 39-57; R. Facelina 'Une Théologie en situation: approche méthodologique' *Revue des Sciences Religieuses* 48 (1974) 311-321.

PART I

Present-day Problems about Jesus, Son of God

Brian McDermott

Jesus Christ in Today's Faith and Theology

THE CONFESSION of Jesus of Nazareth as Son of God, Lord and Christ is today, as it has been for 2,000 years, the hallmark of Christianity and its lifeblood. The New Testament gives expression to this conviction of the identity of the Jesus of the earthly ministry with the heavenly Son of God by means of titles, kerygmatic formulas, and narratives. This New Testament faith in Jesus as Christ and Son of God has been a constant in the 2,000 years of Christian history, but it has always been internally shaped and coloured by the human concerns of each cultural epoch, as people sought for salvation and wholeness from God in Christ in relation to their own deepest and most widely-shared interests and hopes.

Today's human concerns shape Christology in a way peculiar to the late twentieth century. The thirst for personal religious experience, the hunger for social and political justice, the meeting of the world religions, the psychological, sociological and cybernetic-technological revolutions have all exercised their considerable influence on Christology in the university and seminary as well as in the lives of Christians, from middle-class Americans meeting in parishes to Third World members of basic communities often coming together at risk to their lives.

The interaction between popular piety and academic theology is a complicated one, with the theologian sometimes outdistancing the community's expression of its faith (as is the case, for example, of the early stages of the biblical renewal), while at other times, the people of God have developed forms of life which theologians then need to learn from (as, for example, in the renewed sense of the Holy Spirit in Catholic charismatic movements). In this article, I shall explore, in breadth rather than in depth, the sense of Jesus Christ alive in various Christian arenas of life, as well as the directions that the newer Christological efforts of an academic nature are inviting us to follow.

1. JESUS, THE SON OF GOD, IN CONTEMPORARY RELIGIOUS EXPERIENCE

Massive shifts have been occurring in the lives of Christians in recent decades which have both challenged and stimulated their experience of Jesus Christ as the centre of their lives. One can conveniently distinguish these shifts on the levels of person, community and relation to the world.

The personal relation of Christians to Christ has been deeply affected on the grass-roots level by the awakening of a hunger for personal religious experience, which accompanied, paradoxically, the changing cultural patterns of post-industrial western Europe, North America and the so-called 'developing' nations. Where structures no longer satisfactorily mediated a sense of belonging to and being nourished by the Whole, the individual heart sought for meaning in a relationship to God in Christ that was nameable, capable of giving affective sustenance and less dependent on the opinions and experiences of others. The startling increase in directed retreats in the spirit of Ignatian and other religious traditions, the increasing interest on the part of laypeople as well as religious in on-going spiritual direction and the eruption of charismatic prayer groups in which individuals find 'permission' for a life of prayer that allows room for affect, for intimacy in the Spirit, and for a generally more wholistic and healing spiritual attitude are indications that our age is as religious as it is secular. The twin ontological dynamisms in all human beings—to be special and individual on the one hand, and to surrender to the life-giving Other as well—continue to find directly religious expression as well as outlets in psychotherapeutic and other less forthrightly religious ways. Christ has become a real person for many who let themselves pray in the prayer that is all along being given to them in their deepest being.

Renewal of the liturgy, where this has truly succeeded, has awakened Christians to the pivotally communal dimension of Christian living. Here the personal Christ is experienced as the one who can point to his own people and say: 'This is my body for you' (1 Cor. 11:24). The social Christ is not a figure juxtaposed to the personal Christ for those who have known healthy liturgy, but the one Christ experienced in the relationships he enjoys in the Spirit thanks to the resurrection of his body.

A second way in which Christians are newly experiencing Christ is in the widespread sense of call to ministry (once marked off as 'apostolate', 'Catholic Action' and 'vocation'), which is reshaping, gradually but significantly, the landscape in the Church. Participation in Christ's ministry to his Church is increasing among the baptised in an extraordinary degree and the older division of labour does not express or provide adequate guidelines for this development. The empowerment experienced in this call is providing for many members of the Church an opportunity to know Christ in new ways: in his strategies with people of differing needs, in his dedication to the Father's kingdom and his joyful ownership of his Spirit-charged gifts.

Community is developing people's consciousness of Christ in yet a third, closely connected way. The 'basic communities' which are already shaping the Church to come are contexts which allow believers to experience what redaction criticism has told scholars: that each community within the Church has its own experience of God in Christ and is offered the chance to formulate in word and deed (and under grace) its own 'fifth Gospel' which gives names to Christ and to the community just as, for example, Matthew titled Jesus and described the pattern of his life in relation to a particular communal experience of his presence in the Spirit.

If intimacy and community of discipleship are two basic dimensions of Christian experience of Christ, the third component flows out of and reinforces these two. Ministry to the world through mission and witness is that personal and institutional self-forgetfulness which attempts, in collaboration with the labouring Christ and in co-operation with all men and women of good will to humanise the world torn by hunger, poverty and oppression. Ministry to institutions as well as persons quite apart from a view to proselytism; protest at the ravaging of our earth-home; encounter with other world religions to find ways to call all people to belong to this world as the non-divine place where the Mystery can be met and surrendered to, are all ways in which this mission and witness takes on flesh. The Christ-mystery comes to be experienced as larger than this man from Nazareth, while not denying his particularity; liberation becomes a title of central importance and freedom a name for his deepest identity between God and people. No one can say ahead of time what the meeting of the world religions will do to Christians' sense of Jesus in relation to God the Father, the Holy Spirit and to our gradually more common history. No theologian can predict how the growing ecological and socio-political engagement of Christians will affect their consciousness of Christ as the year 2,000 draws near, for that consciousness is in its infancy, and ministry to earth and human world in this post-industrial epoch is in a sense only beginning.

2. RECENT DEVELOPMENTS IN CHRISTOLOGY

The depth and variety of scholarly offerings in the area of Christology presently available to the reading public testify to the renascence which this central area of systematic theology has undergone in the past twenty years. The context of this renewal is partly found in the new freedom of inquiry experienced by Catholic biblical scholars and encouraged by Pius XII's *Divino Afflante Spiritu* (1945) and the Second Vatican Council's Dogmatic Constitution on Divine Revelation (*Dei Verbum*). The explosion of patristic and liturgical studies, of research in the history of doctrine, and investment in wider philosophical options which go far beyond the traditional scholastic philosophies, have also played their role in making the Christological scene as vibrant as it is today. Thanks to the influence of this enriching context, Christology did not develop twenty years ago in the direction which was quite possible for it, that of ever more subtle reflection on the ontological nature of the hypostatic union and of the relations of the trinitarian persons in connection with the incarnation of the Logos.

In surveying some of the aspects of contemporary Christology I shall first offer some summary reflections on method and then select certain salient themes which give focus to the work of many Christologists at the present.

(a) Methods

One of the most striking methodological characteristics of contemporary Christology, both Catholic and Protestant, has been the close relationship between fundamental theology and dogmatic or systematic Christology. Issues of history, evidence and sources and matters of directly doctrinal significance often illumine each other at the hands of, for example, Wolfhart Pannenberg and Karl Rahner.[1] The credibility of the message of Christianity and faith's content are not compartmentalised but recognised as needing to be explored in their reciprocal relationship, while avoiding at the same time the old polemical tones of classical apologetics. Among Catholics, this kind of fundamental-doctrinal Christology is developed as an integral and substantive portion of the theologian's exploration of the meaning of Christian identity (as, for example, we find in Hans Küng and Frans Jozef van Beeck[2]); the relation of science and faith, on the other hand, is the context within which Teilhard de Chardin offers his fresh and controversial interpretation of the Christ-mystery.[3] Modern men and women in their search for meaning for their lives can trace, with Edward Schillebeeckx, the route taken by the first followers of Jesus and the earliest communities of post-Easter believers in their interpretive experiences of salvation from God in Christ which lie at the foundations of the tradition of faith.[4] Sebastian Moore explores the religious and psychological processes by which the believer comes to recognise salvation through the Crucified One and the divine sonship of the Risen One.[5] A mainline Christology such as Walter Kasper's is concerned to relate Christology to the middle-European quest for freedom and unity-in-diversity as he develops a sonship-Christology that is at the same time a Spirit-Christology.[6] The list could easily be continued.

The three most prominent methodologies among Catholic theologians at present are the transcendental method of Karl Rahner, the practical-fundamental theology of

Johannes Baptist Metz,[7] and the praxis-oriented theologies emanating from Latin America. While by no means exhausting the methodological options available at the present time, these three approaches are the major dialogue partners which have claim on our attention.

Metz's practical-fundamental theology has not developed as yet into a systematic Christology but there is evidence of some of the directions which it would take. Emphasis on the healthily subversive role of memory, narrative and hope in relation to universal-historical theories of the world or technocratic and positivistic approaches to the role of humans in history would permit Metz to develop a Christology which would not attempt a theoretical completeness but will again and again interrupt the 'rounding-off' of the human in a way which denies humankind's transcendence towards God and the neighbour in need.

More systematically developed are the Christologies which embody the transcendental method and the liberation method. The former, represented principally by Karl Rahner, involves an investigation of the most basic dimensions of human existence as an existence in knowledge, freedom and love, which are given *a priori* to all particular, categorical experiences. The apriority of our capacity to be conscious, free and loving is discerned in our concrete lives in which we find ourselves already aware and committed, but the uncovering of the basic dimensions or 'existentials' of our historical existence allow the theologian to trace the relationships between the Christian message as a saving message and the reality of the humanity addressed by that message. The transcendental method in the theology of Karl Rahner is never purely transcendental, but its hallmark consists in the constancy with which the human is explored as that worldly reality which already, at least implicitly, experiences God and in this experience is able to experience self, the neighbour and the world. The 'modernist' attempt earlier in the century to show the intrinsic links between humanity's quest for wholeness and divine revelation was abortive; the transcendental method in contemporary theology is a healthier, more mature effort to succeed where 'modernism' failed.

Liberation theology, while learning much from transcendental theology, sees itself as a correction of much of that earlier approach.[8] Theology for these Christians begins with faith, to be sure, but with a faith that is incarnated in a bias, a partiality, in favour of the oppressed. In line with this perspective, the role of the pre-Easter Jesus gains prominence in so far as his praxis in relation to the kingdom (a deeply social symbol) and on behalf of the religiously and socially marginated reveals the structural as well as personal thrust of his mission. His death and resurrection are conceived as political as well as religious in their significance, in so far as it is *this* person with *this* praxis who is executed and is vindicated by God and given a new body in this world in the power of the Spirit.

Rather than emphasising the *a priori* structures of human existence, liberation theology gives central attention to its *a posteriori* elements which threaten human life and society: neo-colonialism, developmental economics, authoritarian régimes, oppressive military and political conspiracies favouring the wealthy, and so forth. The prominent roles of denunciation as well as annunciation, of the study of conflict as well as peace, and of the analysis of class struggle with the aid of Marxist sociology arise not from a merely theoretical appreciation of the value of these concerns, but from the fact that Christians are living out their commitment to Christ in ways which necessitate precisely these forms of reflection for the sake of engaged praxis.[9]

(b) Themes

Contemporary Christologies abound in theological themes which, because of their multiplicity, force one to do some selecting. In order to suggest leading motifs and their inter-connection, rather than trying to be exhaustive I shall choose themes according to a threefold arrangement: themes dealing with the theology of the pre-Easter Jesus, themes having to do with Jesus' resurrection, and finally, motifs that bear on the post-Easter Jesus present in Church and world.

In exploring the significance of the pre-Easter Jesus, theologians have given special attention to (*a*) Jesus the Son of God, (*b*) Jesus the prophet and (*c*) the death of the Son and prophet. I shall look briefly at each of these developments.

In calling the God of Israel 'Abba' Jesus was exposing a revolutionary sense of the nearness of the saving God to himself and those called to share with Jesus in salvation; at the same time he was making an implicit assertion about his own identity as God's Son. Sonship as implicitly asserted by Jesus involved both election or divine favour and communion in life with God, so that Jesus' status is a matter of both grace and nature, as later theology has elaborated. The identity of Jesus as Son is a responsive and receptive identity *vis-à-vis* the Father, and emphasis is placed on the fact that Jesus is first recipient of God's offer of salvation (God's self-communication) before becoming the offer of salvation to others. The totality of his acceptance will be accomplished in the Paschal Mystery, when he receives the divine gift absolutely and so can share the Spirit of his sonship with others. The Son enacts his identity in obedience and faith, and by that obedience and faith we are saved.

If Jesus' sonship summarises for contemporary theologians the ideas of God's closeness, Jesus' election and share in God's being, and his identity as recipient of God's salvation in obedience and faith, his status as prophet, or more specifically, eschatological prophet, makes strikingly clear that Jesus, precisely because of his intimate relationship with the real God (as distinct from the god-*imago* of our ideal self), imagined both God and himself in terms of kingdom, that profoundly social symbol which summed up the longings of Israel for redemption and communion. Jesus both stood in the line of the great prophets of old and was the one through whom the kingdom (i.e., God's salvation) was definitively occurring. As prophet, Jesus presented God to his people and his people to the God who had drawn absolutely near. Like Moses, he beheld God 'face to face' and on the strength of that relationship could offer salvation to individuals and to the religio-political structures of his day. Healing and confrontation marked his ministry as he parabolically spoke and enacted with power the kingdom he obediently sought to anticipate. Contemporary theologians are keenly aware of the rhythm of strength and vulnerability which characterised his service of the kingdom; the kingdom did not emanate out of Jesus' own centre, but came to him and through him to others from the Father who held sway over him. His strength was most effective when he was most receptive of the Father's life and of the reality of those to whom he offered God's gift of acceptance, forgiveness and communion. This openness would be consummated in his death when he would become the 'tent of meeting' between God and sinners.

The death of the Son and prophet is present in much contemporary Christology as a question of Jesus' understanding of his own death. The older dogmatic question of Jesus' self-consciousness here takes on a specificity that would surprise many Christians. Yet the data in the New Testament bearing on Jesus' own sense of his death are slim, once critical methods are applied to the sources. Jesus hoped that the kingdom would be inaugurated through the people's acceptance of his preaching. His death was not part of his 'programme' but the consequence and (as later reflection uncovers) the consummation of his ministry to others in God's name. The eschatological tribulations attendant on the kingdom's arrival which apocalyptic literature emphasises become the lot of Jesus: salvation can come fully to our world only if the violence which is sin is fully encountered by divine love in human form.

One of the most secure convictions of contemporary Christology is the centrality of

Jesus' resurrection for the New Testament and present-day faith. A convenient, if partial, arrangement of the issues can be arrived at if we consider (i) the diversity of traditions; (ii) the first disciples' foundational experience, and (iii) the constitutive role of the resurrection for Jesus' own identity.

The distinction between the tomb-traditions and the appearance-traditions has become a standard element of contemporary Christology, thanks to the results of form-critical and historical-critical analysis of the New Testament texts. A further distinction has been made between the Easter experience of the disciples and the models in which that experience was expressed, only one of which was the appearance model. For many Christians the appearances of the risen Lord are identified with the reality of the resurrection in a way which makes the founding of the Church an empirical rather than a faith event. A distinction between experience, revelation and interpretation can allow the Christian community to appreciate the difference *and* continuity between the experience of the first disciples and later generations of Christians. This theme is a good example of how closely together theologians are keeping fundamental and systematic issues in Christology, since the origin of Easter faith is inseparable from its content and truth.

The distinctions just alluded to put into relief the religious experience of the first disciples, and it is imperative that Christians recognise in the 'founding experiences' the basic elements which will come to explicit light only in the following centuries. The experience of Jesus as God's salvation at the very beginning of the post-Easter community was an experience of the crucified one as being and doing for the disciples what only God can be and do: offer forgiveness of their sins and welcome them into the divine life. The divine sonship of Jesus will become the official understanding of the Church only at the Council of Nicaea (325) but it was implied in the first encounter with Jesus after his death. In the first disciples salvation in its definitive form was accepted for the first time as coming from the risen and exalted one who had been rejected by his people. With them the beginning of the full history of salvation occurred: the age of the Church.

But Easter is not simply a matter of the disciples' transformation. Jesus died into resurrection, and in the power of God's Spirit Jesus, rejected by sinners, was given definitively and absolutely the life he had surrendered to the Father and had rendered vulnerable to the power of sin. Made Lord and Christ (Acts 2:36) by the resurrection, Jesus is made totally present at the Father's right hand and fully present to the world. He now is the kingdom in person, and the Son who shares fully the glory of the Father, the vindicated eschatological prophet. Sometimes theologians speak of the resurrection as having retroactive force with respect to the pre-Easter life of Jesus, but more frequently Easter is portrayed as the confirmation and eschatological transformation of Jesus, gaining content from who Jesus came to be through his life and death and from the glory God shared with him completely in the Spirit at his exaltation.

In later Christology the contrast between the pre-Easter and post-Easter Jesus shifted to a distinction between human nature and divine nature, reflecting the influence of Greek culture on the expanding Christian faith. Three ways in which this shift is critically examined in present-day Christology bear on (i) the pre-existence and personhood of Jesus Christ, (ii) the personal and social lordship of Christ and (iii) the relation between theology and worship.

The pre-existence of Jesus as God's eternal Son is a Jewish and Hellenistic way of expressing the saving significance of Jesus. Mythic in its manner of expression, the concept has persisted because of the recognition that Jesus shares in God's pre-existence *vis-à-vis* the created order. Contemporary Christologists have discussed the concept in its relation to the resurrection, in its Jewish apocalyptic roots and its Greek development. In what sense the eternal Son or Word is *personally* pre-existent is a matter of dispute with the suggestion being made that the eternal Word be thought of more as a mode of being than as a person apart from the incarnation.[10] The reason for this suggestion is partly grounded in the desire to allow the human reality of Jesus to be fully personal precisely as human, a proposal which in some of its formulations can appear to conflict with the more traditional view that Jesus is a human person by virtue of his human nature's rootedness in the second person of the Trinity. The Chalcedonian and neo-Chalcedonian formulas which provide the basis for much later reflection on the hypostatic union are now the object of critical rethinking precisely to allow the affirmations of faith to give full scope to the unity of Jesus Christ and his full consubstantiality with God and ourselves.

The personal identity of Christ, now fully present to God and the world, is an identity of lordship which touches the most intimate core of persons and the most complex social webs which shape, express, unite and divide us. The social lordship of Jesus (which can only be believed and experienced in the Spirit) is a theme which is central to political and liberation theologies, which make great efforts to hold close together a theology of creation and a theology of redemption. As Genesis 1-11 make clear, God's creative work continues in the civilising efforts of humans, and Jesus' ministry as risen Lord is the eschatological source of challenge and transformation for human structures as well as human hearts bound by oppressive forces. The relation of Jesus to the 'culture of pluralism', to world religions, to the corporate life of business and the conflicts between affluent nations and the Third World motifs which engage the minds and imaginations of theologians as they defend the hope that is in them for our world in all its created complexity, its sin and grace.

Healthy theology is bound to faith's most complete and embodied enactment: worship and witness. It is here that the primary language of faith ('Christ is risen') is uttered as response to experienced presence, and it is here that the narratives of faith are most 'hearable'. Thus the renewed awareness of the primacy of the resurrection in Christology has led theologians to reunite theology, worship and the *imitatio Christi*. At the same time, the narrative shape of Christology, and indeed of all Christian theology, has received fresh attention, since the Christian message can be authentically expressed in theology by a metaphysics only if that metaphysics stands in a healthy, tensive relationship to narrative, through which personal and communal identity can be critically and nourishingly proclaimed and enacted.

Notes

1. W. Pannenberg *Jesus-God and Man* (Philadelphia [2]1977) (*Grundzüge der Christologie*, Gütersloh [3]1969); K. Rahner *Foundations of Christian Faith, An Introduction to the Idea of Christianity* (New York 1978) (*Grundkurs des Glaubens: Einführung in den Begriff des Christentums*, Freiburg im Breisgau 1976).

2. H. Küng *On Being a Christian* (Garden City, NY 1974) (*Christ Sein*, München 1974); F. J. van Beeck *Christ Proclaimed, Christology as Rhetoric* (New York 1979).

3. See C. F. Mooney *Teilhard de Chardin and the Mystery of Christ* (New York 1966).

4. E. Schillebeeckx *Jesus, An Experiment in Christology* (New York 1979) (*Jezus, het verhaal van een levende*, Bloemendaal [3]1975).

5. S. Moore *The Crucified Jesus Is No Stranger* (New York 1977); *The Fire and the Rose Are One* (New York 1980).

6. W. Kasper *Jesus the Christ* (New York 1976) (*Jesus der Christus*, Mainz 1974).

7. J.-B. Metz *Faith in History and Society, Toward a Practical Fundamental Theology* (New York 1980) (*Glaube in Geschichte und Gesellschaft*, Mainz 1977).

8. J. Sobrino *Christology at the Crossroads, A Latin American Approach* (Maryknoll, NY 1978) (*Christologia desde america latina*, Mexico 1976); L. Boff *Jesus Christ Liberator* (Maryknoll, NY 1978) (*Jesus Christo Liberator*, Petrópolis, Brazil 1972).

9. Compare the European Marxist approach to Christ in M. Machoveĉ *A Marxist Looks at Jesus* (Philadelphia 1976) (*Jesus für Atheisten*, Stuttgart 1972).

10. See P. Schoonenberg *The Christ, A Study of the God-Man Relationship in the Whole of Creation and in Jesus Christ* (New York 1971) (*Hij is een God van Mensen*, 's-Hertogenbosch 1969). The more recent British debate concerning the Incarnation is represented by *The Myth of God Incarnate* ed. J. Hick (Philadelphia 1977).

Nicholas Lash

'Son of God': Reflections on a Metaphor

1. IS IT REALLY TRUE?

RECENT DEBATES concerning the availability for contemporary use of the concept of 'incarnation' suggest that something like the following exchange could take place between an inquiring Christian and any one of a number of well-known theologians. Inquirer: ' "Jesus is the Son of God"; true or false?'. Theologian: 'Before I can answer, I need to consider a prior question which the early Christians failed to consider because they lacked our sophisticated modern awareness of the differences between various types of linguistic usage. I need to consider whether it is being asserted that Jesus is literally, or only metaphorically, the Son of God. As a purported literal description, the proposition is either unintelligible or, if intelligible, false. It is true, but only metaphorically true, that Jesus is the Son of God.'

Our inquirer now raises another question: 'Is the proposition "God exists" true or false?'. And this time the theologian (who is himself a believer) answers, unhesitatingly, 'true'. The inquirer (who has learnt a thing or two from the previous exchange) now asks: 'But is the proposition "God exists" literally or only metaphorically true?'. To this question, most of those theologians who were quite confident that the proposition 'Jesus is the Son of God' is only metaphorically true would now show themselves equally confident that the proposition 'God exists' is literally true.

At this point, a third party (another theologian, perhaps myself) joins the conversation and says that he believes the proposition 'God exists' to be true, but that it is metaphorically rather than literally true. To this suggestion, the theologian who displayed his fearless capacity for 'radical' thought in resolutely asserting that the proposition 'Jesus is the Son of God' is only metaphorically true, now reacts with some nervousness: 'But if the proposition "God exists" is only metaphorically true, then it is not *really* true that God exists'. And he suspects the third party not only of unorthodoxy (which would not trouble him) but of atheism (which would). And the latecomer would probably be accused of confusing rather than clarifying things if he said that it would only follow, from the denial that the statement 'God exists' is literally true, that God does not really exist, if the concept of 'God' functions as a proper name which, in Christian theology, it does not.

In this article, I wish to offer some reflections on one or two issues raised by that little

11

exchange.[1] In view of the complexity of these issues, I can only do so in a very impressionistic manner. (Thus, for example, I willingly admit that to employ a 'strategic' distinction between the 'literal' and the 'metaphorical' is crudely to oversimplify a number of fundamental issues in linguistics and the philosophy of language. Nevertheless, in view of the fact that just such a distinction has been widely appealed to in recent theological debates, I thought it might be useful to accept it but to attempt, as it were, to 'stand it on its head'.) I wish to suggest that the proposition 'Jesus is the Son of God' is true; that if it were false, Christian hope would be deprived of its grounds and Christian faith of its object; that, while 'divine sonship' is, indeed, predicated metaphorically of Jesus, it does not follow that he is not 'really' the Son of God; and that although Christian uses of the concept of 'God' are *also* metaphorical in character, it does not thereby follow that it is not 'really' true that God exists.

2. METAPHOR, MEANING AND HOPE

There are philosophical traditions in which it is confidently assumed, firstly, that the distinction between literal and metaphorical uses of language is (in principle) unproblematic; secondly, that the central and primary function of language is to make straightforward descriptive statements (and that to deny or even to question this view is to open the floodgates to 'subjectivism' and unrestrained 'relativism'); thirdly, that the further language moves from the canonical standard of literal description (by metaphorical 'extension', for example) the more suspect its objectivity, clarity and capacity unambiguously to express the truth; fourthly, that all metaphoric discourse is, in some straightforward sense, false, and that the truth which the metaphor indirectly states can always be directly stated in non-metaphorical terms.

All these assumptions, I suggest, are highly questionable. Quite apart from the arbitrary philistinism which would consign most of the world's poetic, dramatic and literary discourse to some limbo of 'merely expressive', non-cognitive ambiguity and imprecision, such a view of language paradoxically venerates 'scientific' discourse as the ideal of literal description at a time when philosophers of science increasingly draw attention to the extent to which the language of natural science is saturated with metaphor.

I am not denying the importance of distinctions between literal and metaphorical discourse. Nor am I denying that there are situations in which that distinction is drawn without difficulty (if, for example, I am told that it is 'raining cats and dogs', I do not look out of the window expecting to see the street outside littered with fallen bodies). Nevertheless, I wish, firstly, to insist that appropriate judgments in such matters are the fruit of practical linguistic competence rather than matter for more or less arbitrary *a priori* stipulation; and, secondly, to explore the possibility that it may nevertheless be helpful to attribute primacy to metaphorical rather than to literal usage.

Human existence is a matter of transforming, or seeking to transform, our circumstances; a matter of making ourselves at home, or of making a home for ourselves; a matter of transforming cosmos into environment. In this process, linguistic activity plays a central and indispensable role. Our struggle to 'make sense' of the world is a quest for meaning: an attempt to discern, construct and transform the meaning of things. This, I think, is what Cornelius Ernest had in mind when, not unaware of the reasons why some philosophers have warned us that it may be misleading to speak of 'meaning' as an 'activity', he nevertheless described 'meaning' as 'primarily a praxis by which the world to which man belongs becomes the world which belongs to man'.[2]

On this account, primacy is attributed to the *transformative* potential of human action, including linguistic action. 'It is not the extension of language, by metaphor or in any other way, which is the puzzle. It is literalness which needs to be explained.'[3] We are a people on pilgrimage, a people in quest both of a home and of an identity. We have not yet succeeded in making ourselves, or in making a home for ourselves. And, because we have not, it is the stability, transparency and security of the 'literal' which is fragile, fitful, threatened and often questionable. It is, for example, an illusion to suppose that, merely because we can and must specify as exactly as possible our uses of the term 'human', we can give a 'literal' description of the meaning of humanity, of what it is or might be to be fully human: an illusion which supposes that we have achieved the goal, the identity, the self-understanding, which we seek.

We cannot 'literally' depict ultimate goals. As we seek, through transformative action, to open up and realise the possibilities, the most we can do is to indicate, metaphorically, what they might be 'like'. But the possibilities are not unlimited. There are boundaries and constraints beyond which we may not reasonably hope and profitably strive. Beyond these boundaries, the most formidable of which appears to be the barrier of mortality (the mortality alike of the individual and of the species), there lies not hope but fantasy.

It is at this point that the question of the rationality of human hope becomes, at one and the same time, the question of God and the question of man's resurrection.

That conclusion was reached with suspicious rapidity. We must now go back to the beginning and approach the matter by a different route.

3. GOD

In suggesting, as I did at the beginning, that the statement 'God exists' is to be understood metaphorically, I do not mean to imply that God may only metaphorically be said to 'exist', but that, having no proper name for that which, in this statement, we affirm to exist, we make do with the metaphorical expression 'God', an expression inherited from a long and complex history of religious practice and reflection.

The central question here concerns whether or not the term 'God' functions, in Christian religious and theological discourse, as a proper name. The centrality of forms of *address* in religious discourse may give the impression that 'God' is the proper name of him to whom we cry, whom we praise, adore and celebrate. This impression, however, is misleading. After all, we often address human beings without using their names: 'my brother'; 'Mr President'; 'my love'. Similarly, I suggest that the term 'God' functions as a title or description rather than as a proper name.

Most religious traditions have supposed idolatry to be both possible and reprehensible. Idolatry is the worship of a false god. The very possibility of distinguishing, or attempting to distinguish, between 'true gods' and 'false gods' suggests that the word 'god' is a description rather than a name.

But could we not say that 'God' is the proper name of the only true 'god'? Quite apart from the fact that this would be a somewhat confusing recommendation, the history of Christian extensions or transformations of Jewish and Greek concepts of divinity hardly points in this direction. Nor is it easy to see how a description, a '*nomen naturae*', becomes a proper name merely in virtue of the fact that there is only one to whom this description truly refers. We *might* say that, in the New Testament, 'God' functions 'rather like' a proper name, not in so far as the true God is distinguished from false gods, but in so far as the term is used to distinguish the Father from his Son and Spirit. However, 'Father', 'Son' and 'Spirit' are not proper names either.[4]

If 'God' were taken to be a proper name, what would be the appropriate general term to describe the relationship between 'God', 'Gott', 'Dieu', 'Yahweh' or 'Allah'? In at least some of these cases the term 'translation' would be inappropriate (and, anyway, in what sense do we usually 'translate' proper names?). Are these words, as it were, 'aliases'? And how would we know? In the case of human beings, we are able to establish whether different proper names refer to the same person inasmuch as the person is identifiable, not only by description, but also by direct or indirect acquaintance. We do not, however, know God by acquaintance, but only by description. (Or perhaps it would be better to say that, in so far as a Christian *does* suppose himself to know God as an acquaintance who can be named, his name is Jesus Christ.)

I am suggesting that 'God' is a description and not a proper name, and that to believe that God exists is not to believe something or other about God, but to believe that there is something or other which has divine attributes. It is to believe that divine attributes have reference.

The question, then, is not: what can we predicate of 'God'? but rather: what do we take to be 'divine' attributes? To ask an individual, or a group, what attributes they take to be divine is to ask them what they take to be of ultimate reality and significance. It is to ask them where they ultimately put their trust; on what their hearts and hopes are set.

The answers will vary considerably and from that variety have sprung enduring and intractable human conflicts—cultural, political and religious. Concerning this vast topic, I wish only to make four points. Firstly, the term 'God' functions, in practice, as short-hand for some particular set of divine attributes. Secondly, the proposition 'God exists' is, logically, a confessional, 'self-involving' utterance. It declares, and the declaration is heavy with the risk of illusion and idolatry, that such-and-such are divine attributes and that these attributes have reference: that there is that on which it is appropriate thus to set all our trust, all our hope. Thirdly, those attributes we take to be divine are not mere ideas or ideals, but features of ultimate and, in that sense, transcendent reality. And, fourthly, it needs to be added (in the shadow of Feuerbach and Durkheim) that that to which such attributes refer is not reducible to any actual or possible feature or set of features of nature or history.

The suggestion that all attempts to speak of God are metaphorical, that they express (however imperfectly) the deepest convictions of those who make such language their own concerning the character and outcome of that transformative (creative and redemptive) process in which they, and others, are engaged in seeking to make sense of things, affords not the slightest licence for self-indulgence or imprecision. The crucial question is not whether we can speak of God 'literally', but whether we can speak of God truthfully. And, in our attempts to speak truthfully of God, we do not lack all criteria of appropriateness. But, for the Christian, questions of criteria are questions of Christology, to which we now turn.

4. SON OF GOD

Two preliminary points. In the first place, there is no reason to suppose that Christians in the early centuries were unable to distinguish between primary and secondary, 'focal' or extended, uses of words, nor that they necessarily took the concept of 'sonship' to refer only or even primarily to physical descent and relationship.[5]

In the second place, some modern philosophers of religion proceed on the assumption that Christological propositions furnish 'additional information' concerning a God whose general identifying characteristics have been antecedently ascertained. Historically, it seems more correct to say that the forging of Christological and trinitarian language expressed the attempt to *transform* inherited concepts of 'God' in the light of reflection on him who was confessed as 'Son' of God and on the mystery which, even in agony, he addressed as 'Father'.

In the light of these preliminary remarks, what are we to make of the notion of 'divine sonship'?

Jesus was, as we all are, a product of nature and history. As such a product, he was destructible and was, indeed, destroyed. We are none of us, however, *merely* 'products'. We are not merely produced; we are also, in different ways and with most varying efficacy, *cherished*. There are few human beings of whom someone has not, at some time, even fleetingly, been fond.

But, quite apart from the fact that many people are little loved, and loved with little selfishness and effective care, even the purest and most effective human loving cannot prevent the destruction, cannot transcend the mortality, of the products that we are.

To declare Jesus to be the Son of God is, I suggest, to declare that he was not only produced, but effectively, indestructibly, 'absolutely' cherished. If we take 'loving production' to be part of what we mean by 'true parenthood', and if, in declaring Jesus to be the Son of *God*, we declare 'parenthood' to be a divine attribute, then we are thereby declaring our conviction, derived from reflection on his fate, that being lovingly produced, being effectively cherished with a love that transcends destruction in mortality, is an aspect of what it ultimately is, means and will be to be human.

I suggested, in the previous section, that 'God exists' is a confessional utterance. I am now suggesting that 'Jesus is the Son of God' is, similarly, a confessional utterance, declaring our faith in his resurrection and our hope for the resurrection of all mankind. If 'parenthood' is a divine attribute, then the destruction of the product is not the last word concerning the human condition.

Two final comments. Firstly, the anthropomorphism which seduces us into treating 'God' as a proper name has sometimes misled Christians into supposing that, if Jesus is truly God's Son, then he cannot also be (for example) Joseph's son. But this is simply a mistake. To declare Jesus to be the Son of *God* does not entail the denial that he was any other father's son.

Secondly, it is worth noting that, in confessing Jesus to be 'Son of God', it is 'parenthood', rather than either 'paternity' or 'maternity', which is declared to be a divine attribute.

5. CONCLUSION

Martin Hengel has described 'Son of God' as 'an established, unalienable metaphor of Christian theology'.[6] I have done no more, in this brief sketch, than to suggest that if this 'title' is not to be misunderstood as a piece of outmoded mythology, then it is on questions concerning the logic of the concept of 'God', and on questions concerning the character of the quest for human identity, fulfilment and self-understanding, that we should concentrate attention.

We seek so to transform our circumstances and our understanding as to make the world to which we belong a world which belongs to us.

To be able to say, in the face of human suffering and mortality, of the non-achievement of human meaning and the darkness of the future, that Jesus is *truly* the Son of God, and that therefore we also are and will be 'sons' and 'daughters', is either infantilist escapism or the mature expression of appropriate hope. That confession, I have suggested, declares our hope of resurrection, of that indefeasible transformation of nature and circumstance in which human existence attains its fulfilment and true identity in belonging to God. We can only speak truly in metaphors concerning that of which the new Jerusalem which we seek will be, we might say, the 'literal' expression.

Notes

1. For the debates referred to in the opening paragraph, see, e.g. *The Myth of God Incarnate* ed. J. Hick (London 1977); *Incarnation and Myth: The Debate Continued* ed. M. Goulder (London 1979). As random illustrations of the assumptions summarised in the first paragraph of the section on 'Metaphor', assumptions which reflect a particular strand of positivism in British philosophy, see D. Cupitt *Taking Leave of God* (London 1980) p. 122; R. Trigg *Reason and Commitment* (London 1973). On the ontology of metaphor sketched in that section, see C. Ernst *Multiple Echo: Explorations in Theology* (London 1979); 'Meaning and Metaphor in Theology' *New Blackfriars* 61 (1980) 100-112. For the account of the logical status of the concept of 'God' in the section on 'God', see P. Geach *God and the Soul* (London 1969) pp. 57-59, 100-116.

2. C. Ernst *Multiple Echo* p. 55.

3. C. Ernst 'Meaning and Metaphor in Theology' 109.

4. On this point of logic I must disagree with Claude Geffré, in his interesting article ' "Father" as the Proper Name of God' *Concilium* 143 (1981) 43.

5. See M. Hengl *The Son of God* (London 1976) p. 21.

6. *Ibid.* pp. 92-93.

Dietrich Wiederkehr

'Son of God' and 'Sons of God': The Social Relevance of the Christological Title

IT IS not only in the field of liberation theology that theologians and Christians look sceptically and suspiciously at one another according to which of two tendencies they follow. This happens too in the theology and in the church life of western Europe. Those who champion the Church's doctrinal tradition want to know that the dogmatic formulations of the early Church are being strictly preserved, and many attempts at re-interpretation arouse in them the suspicion that the previous heritage of faith will be lost for the sake of an immediate practical advantage. On the other side many convinced and committed Christians in the course of living out their faith either as individuals or in relation to society break out of the linguistic confines of dogma in order to liberate an understanding and an energy based on Jesus Christ that is in fact closer to what they are doing. On this view describing Jesus as the 'Son of God' is remote from the demands of Christian living and is apolitical if not negatively political, a label which does not provide any encouragement or movement but rather threatens to raise obstacles to practical action for humanity and justice. It is only a Jesus Christ who has smashed the crystalline shell of dogmatic language and who has been liberated from it by force to make a new language and inspiration possible that can be proclaimed meaningfully and responsibly and can be fruitfully incorporated in one's own efforts and concerns. Dogma is a-political or anti-political; the Christian's political activity is a-dogmatic or anti-dogmatic. The two opposing tendencies are not always juxtaposed in such an unpolemical fashion as in the Puebla document: 'Our task is to proclaim the mystery of the incarnation without equivocation' and: 'We must present Jesus in the way he shares the life, hopes and fears of his people' (Puebla 175-176). But is the dogmatic statement about Jesus being the Son of God so unfruitful for social action, and is social action so lacking a sense of tradition that it cannot derive anything from the title 'Son of God'? The reflections that follow are meant to serve mutual rapprochement and a deepening awareness of each other's position. From them critical questions arise both for the official dogmatic doctrinal tradition and for the impatience of the practical Christian.

1. DIVINITY OR DIVINE SONSHIP?

To begin with, the dogmatic understanding of faith needs to retrieve its own contents. A critical review of the history of patristic and scholastic theology will quickly

17

show that, alongside the stress on the divinity belonging to Christ's nature and essence, the term 'Son of God' in Christology remained only a verbal modification without having any marked effect on doctrinal content or the practice of piety. But this meant that the Church's doctrinal tradition deprived itself of various potential energies contained in the tradition of language and faith. Admittedly the Christology of the early Church, with its statements about substance and nature no longer given a personal stamp, does stand within a soteriological and practical context, but the past's experience of the absence of salvation and the expectation of salvation in the form of becoming divine meant that Jesus' *relationship as son* as well as that of the redeemed children of God were ignored and unused. To the same extent there was of course a weakening of the significance that enabled one to conclude from 'Son' to 'brethren' in a way that broadened out to give the latter a share in the former. But this provided, if at first in symbolic form and not yet in the rationalising language of politics, a starting-point for a theoretical and practical interpretation of the Christological description for present-day Christians' experience of the faith and for their living out of their belief. This too provides the continuity; backwards to the Christology of the New Testament in both its implicit and its explicit form, and forwards to the present day and modern Christians' relationship to transcendence that is sometimes hidden and challenged and sometimes conscious and lived out and also to the threatened openness of modern society. If for a proper understanding of the dogma of the early Church and its subsequent continuation and abridgement it is necessary to take one's bearings from the original testimony about Jesus of the New Testament community and its documents, then this very much applies too to the soteriological and practical effects, which can be seen much more clearly in the contexts in which the New Testament applies the title 'Son of God'.

2. THE SOTERIOLOGICAL MOTIVE FOR THE FORMATION OF 'SON' CHRISTOLOGY

The biblical theological reflections that follow are set within the context of contemporary questions and concerns. If situations of the action of salvation directed towards individuals and social groups provide the context for the first formulations of a Christology, then the Christological names and titles that arise from this remain understandable only with this context; then for a subsequent bringing of them into relationship with other and different practical situations does not signify any alienation and functionalisation of the mystery of Christ. This applies even when these situations no longer demonstrate the simple structure of salvation being mediated to a suffering individual or group but are embedded in more complex social structures or are penetrated by them. If it was *from* situations like this that the term 'Son of God' arose, then it can once again be derived and made actual *in* such situations. This cannot be opposed by an intermediate form of Christology (and possibly by dogma itself too) that has possibly distanced itself and moved away from this. It is rather the momentary outcome of the practical context for which amends need to be made. Certainly the term 'Son of God' belongs to that phase in the formation of Christology that occurred only after earlier less explicit indications and characterisations of the person of Jesus within the context of what he said and did. At the start are situations to the interpretation of which the proclamation of the kingdom of God is brought in by Jesus himself: Jesus' own place within these situations is often not really indicated but qualified by the logic of a parable. The elucidations that follow the parable of the vineyard (Matt. 21:33-45) with their more than clear aids to understanding were no doubt preceded by more restrained hints. On the other hand sayings of Jesus implying omnipotence, like the antitheses of the sermon on the mount (Matt. 5:21-48) or the casting out of demons showing that the kingdom of God had come upon his audience (Matt. 12:28), provide the starting-point for further essays in elucidation. In this earliest form of what has been termed implicit

Christology there appears a new unity of action and omnipotence between God and Jesus which does not juxtapose two rival actors but in which Jesus refers himself to God and knows he is given all power by him. The image of the Father and the linguistically original *Abba* mode of address introduce the process of elucidation which will finally (as early as Jesus himself?) lead in the community to the term 'Son of God'. It is not our business here to describe the individual stages of this process. What is important for the questions we are dealing with is *the practical context* from which the term 'Son of God' grew and to which it must remain linked. This *unity of action* between God and Jesus, between the kingdom of God that is breaking in on us and its proclamation here and now and the anticipation of salvation by Jesus, is brought together as in a focal point and concentrated in individual representations of the epiphany. These proclamations are only rightly located as advance indications or the final punctuation of Jesus' individual acts and statements of salvation that come between, just as on the other hand these words of revelation make visible the mystery of the individual situations and actions. The actual settings of the signs of salvation are not so un-Christological, and the Christological proclamations and descriptions are not so lacking in bearing on actual practice. In this way the term 'Son of God' represents *the summary and balance* drawn up from the individual fragments of what Jesus did: the calling of the disciples, the casting out of demons, the radical commitment to the will of God, the meal-fellowship with sinners, etc. The connection between the Christological title 'Son of God' and what Jesus did to help people appears in mirror-image in the mocking call to Jesus on the cross: 'He trusts in God; let God deliver him now, if he desires him; for he said, "I am the Son of God" ' (Matt. 27:43). The relationship is a mutual one: Jesus' assumption of full power with the eschatological claim to judgment as is proper to God, and Jesus' reliance on God's mission and faithfulness. It was on the basis of this tradition of choice that the title was taken up and intensified by the New Testament. It attains its lasting value with the exaltation of the one raised from the dead to the right hand of God, to a position of equal power and majesty.

Several components of this Christology-in-formation dropped out, however, and *got lost* in the later process of reflection and conceptual refinement. On the one hand the dynamic and relational communication of God to Jesus and vice versa increasingly lost its impetus: the conferment of equal power and the factual identification of Jesus with God's own love and will led to the static position of Jesus' uniqueness being based on his divine nature and substance. The categories of nature, substance and essence weakened and limited the category of relationship, and in this the influence of the philosophical and linguistic environment played its part. To the same extent, however, the practical situation that gave rise to the Christological concept 'Son of God' was squeezed out to the margin and finally lost. The mystery of Christ was first made manifest by *action* in relation to others that brought about and laid claim to salvation; now it became a self-contained and indeed *isolated mystery of being*. Moreover, the actual people to whom Jesus spoke and with whom he dealt have become dispensable: both the individuals whom he healed of their afflictions and the groups he gathered together and united across all social barriers. It was *together with other people* that the person of Jesus was made manifest as the locus of sonship in the face of the Father: now he stands for himself alone. The early disqualification of an adoptionist Christology together with the disappearance of the Jewish Christian communities and their theology meant in addition that the dynamic relationship and unity of sonship between Jesus and God was *foreshortened* to the doctrine of the two natures in Christ. The survival of the term 'Son of God' in the creed and in Christology was no longer able to inject its soteriological and practical potential but was instead displaced by the dominant symmetrical Christology of Chalcedon. In this way the *dogmatic statement* was able to encourage the suspicion of being *without soteriological, practical or indeed political relevance*. But originally, on the basis of the New Testament context, this ought not to have been so.

3. THE SON AS SOTERIOLOGICAL PROTOTYPE

In contrast to its subsequent isolation, the term 'Son of God' discloses *a practical dimension* as early as the context of the life of Jesus himself. This expansion becomes stronger and more significant for salvation in the process of reflection on the history of salvation. In the letter to the Galatians (3:26-4:7) a broad area is first sketched out of the human situation of the lack of salvation and freedom, and in the midst of this the Christological description obtains a far-reaching significance. Once again we read the New Testament text *in the perspective of political theology*: the soteriological context of the Christological statement is at the same time a context of the religious and cultural conditions prevailing in society at the time. The text gives the impression that in the forefront of Paul's awareness was at first the contrast between the two human situations, the transition made possible by grace from servitude to freedom and the status of being a son and heir. From the soteriological category he pushes forward to the Christological category, but if it is to be understood aright this latter remains *bound to the situation from which it arose*: what 'Son of God' means must start from and remain related to the sons and daughters who become free men and women and heirs from having been slaves and prisoners. The introduction of the 'Son' establishes the transformation of the situation in a way that is both central and broadening out on the periphery, and does so within a contrast between sin and salvation. What is involved here is not just individual existences marked by the lack of salvation but *structures of unfreedom*: 'under the law' that imposes itself as an all-embracing pattern ordering one's life. Hence in the new order of faith one should see not merely a private new existence of the individual but just as much a *total structure redefinition of the situation*, 'under faith'. The two contrasting structural situations of law and faith find their existential expression in the status of slaves and of sons, in the contrast between the person not yet of age and the heir who has come into his or her inheritance, and in the contrast between subjection to the elements of the world and the fullness of time. The change in this situation that is defined in these various different ways is introduced in the middle of the argument: 'when the time had fully come, God sent forth his Son' (Gal. 4:4). Just as beforehand the concentric circles of the situation of evil were drawn tighter and tighter, now the circles of the new situation of salvation broaden out to redefine the individual and his or her structural situation. On the basis of the Son they are no longer distinguished as Jews and Greeks, slaves and free, male and female, but 'you are all one in Christ Jesus' (Gal. 3:28). This extension and participation is strengthened by the gift of the Spirit, who testifies to and brings about the reality of the new existence and the new structural situation: 'And because you are sons, God has sent the Spirit of his Son into our hearts, crying, "Abba! Father!" So through God you are no longer a slave but a son, and if a son then an heir' (Gal. 4:6-7). There can be no doubt of the *origin* of the Christological title 'Son of God' and what it is directed *towards*: it cannot simply be exploited as an isolated dogmatic statement about Jesus Christ as if a Christological theory could be detached from its contemporary context of the experience of salvation in practical and political terms. Paul was thus able to link the term 'Son of God' with the existing religious and social, and therefore political, situation in an *internal logical relationship*. Hence it seems no less legitimate today and indeed necessary to introduce the term 'Son of God' into contemporary contexts and situations of law and faith, of slavery and freedom. If the practical and social dimension belonged to the historical and biblical understanding of the title of 'Son', then it belongs no less to an authentic tradition and interpretation of this title in the context of contemporary experience and action.

To amplify this we need to look at another complex passage where there is a similar interweaving of statements about man's sinfulness, the change brought about by the new gift of sonship, and the hope for manifest and complete salvation and liberation. If in the letter to the Galatians it was a question of the social structure of law and freedom *that extends beyond the individual*, in that to the Romans (Rom. 8:19-26) it is man's involvement with nature and the world (which in Gal. 4:3, as 'elements of the world', formed part of the enslaving structures). The passage of time and the feeling of impatience are experienced more clearly than in Galatians: already they have received the first fruits of the Spirit and still they are waiting to be fully adopted as sons and for this to be revealed. If the possibilities of shortening this time of waiting are small, so that groaning seems all that is possible, then this groaning will be granted greater strength and effectiveness in consideration of man's contemporary experience of nature and the world. Once again this supra-individual cosmic experience, whether passive or active, whether enduring being enslaved to corruption or hoping for freedom, is placed in a setting centred on Christ: 'For all who are led by the Spirit of God are sons of God . . .; and if children, then heirs, heirs of God and fellow heirs with Christ, provided we suffer with him in order that we may also be glorified with him' (Rom. 8:14, 17). In this the eschatological proviso of the cross sets a limit to a thorough-going cosmic expansion and radiation of the mystery of Christ, but even this side of this limit the status of children in the 'Son of God' demands and promises a universal range: 'For the creation waits with eager longing for the revealing of the sons of God' (Rom. 8:19). If in interpreting Christology in the context of our contemporary experience of nature and of the world, with the ecological dilemmas we face and the efforts to find a solution, recourse is had once again to the central mystery of Christ, this is not extended beyond its potentialities but rather set free to make its original potentialities possible. This applies also when this kind of interpretation and action involves the dull facts and political tensions of destroying and maintaining the environment. The range of salvation in the Son Jesus Christ is not thereby abandoned but rather attained.

4. THE POLITICAL DIMENSION OF SONSHIP IN MYTHOLOGICAL AND RATIONAL SPEECH AND ACTION

In a premature attack on the programme of political theology the deduction was made from the absence of political terminology in the gospels that what Jesus said and did and the life of the early Christian community as well did not have political relevance in mind. This conclusion is superficial from various points of view, as well as when considered in relation to our subject of the title 'Son of God' in a political context then and now.

The effect and significance of what Jesus did and what his young community did thus takes place on foundations interpenetrated by society, even if they do not explicitly advert to and expose these roots but are merely concerned with an individual human being and his or her apparently private affairs. At the latest the reaction to what Jesus did shows that, even in a simple encounter with a leper, with a sick man on the sabbath or in the synagogue, with his new circle of those he ate with, he disturbs and breaks through existing social rules and sees their sanctions descend on him. Applied to our subject, this means that if Jesus' approach to man takes place by way of an anticipatory manifestation of the power of God, and if in this he is acting on the basis of his community and unity of action with the Father, then the sonship that is made explicit later erupts into the world of social structures and critically breaks through the existing order, symbolically and paradigmatically inaugurating a new order.

It was already clear from the biblical theological analysis of the passages in Paul that the change from being a slave to being free and a son does not remain confined to a history that can be restricted to an individual but that *overarching social structures are changed and discarded.* It is valid to see social images that can be compared with and translated into more modern societies in the religiously articulated regulations of the Jewish law and of Christian faith freed from the law. These more modern societies may for their part no longer make use of an explicit religious superstructure, as is the case with the secularised bourgeois or socialist societies of the modern age. If freedom in Christ, sonship with the Son, had at that time tangible effects which included this social sphere, then one will be equally unwilling to restrict the existence of the new man 'in the Son' to an internal religious sphere today. There is certainly a difference between the language of the Bible and contemporary consideration of society. Given the lack of a critical analysis of the various forces involved, there was merely the short-hand of mythological or symbolic language: slavery under the law, being subject to the elements of the world, the ephemeral nature of creation, etc. These are elements that can and must be rationalised but that should not simply be excluded in a total liquidation of mythological language. At the same time the symbolic descriptions of the redeemed social reality call for realisation in practice as already happens or ought to happen. What corresponds to liberation from the law, the doing away with circumcision, being ransomed from the tutelage of the law? The relativisation of the distinctions between Jew and Greek, slave and free, male and female ought not to be left the other side of social discrimination along these lines. This is all the more so in as much as *the possibilities of critical analysis and practical change of structures* are much more extensive than was possible for Paul and his communities. Nor did he tolerate any delay with regard to specifically legal provisions: at least within their community Christians should draw practical consequences which decisively changed their status in religious society as it had existed.

Similarly redeemed sonship in Christ and in his Spirit that has already been received will bring with it more an abstract new attitude and approach towards creation. If the subjection of creation can no longer be aetiologically traced back to Adam but tangible and denotable forces of destruction threaten the living environment, then the groaning of creation must be translated into rational language and political action.

The alienation of Christians from dogmatic Christology or from social action that I mentioned at the beginning can be overcome if both consider the origins: that for Jesus and for the early Christian community 'Son of God' was always situated in a *context of practical and social action*; and that in reverse the new way of Christian action and the alternative offered by the social reality of the Church were understood and realised as the implementation of liberated sonship in and from Jesus Christ. Those who guard *dogmatic faith in Jesus Christ* as 'Son of God' should once again *venture into the actual practical contexts*, as happened when this description took shape; committed Christians should in their active and passive, struggling and reforming discipleship refer back to the foundation that makes it all possible, the 'Son' and their own 'sonship'. The *unity of dogmatic faith and practical action* in the paradigm situations of the Bible does not take away from us the task of seeking this unity today. Indeed, it both demands and promises their convergence.

Translated by Robert Nowell

Note

This article is based on the consensus that can be discerned in dogmatic Christology and the history of Christological dogma. For the New Testament and contemporary context of the description 'Son of God' it takes as its model the analysis of Edward Schillebeeckx, in the section on the New Testament experience of grace and social structures in *Christus und die Christen* (Freiburg 1977) pp. 543-549.

Jon Sobrino

A Crucified People's Faith in the Son of God

THIS ARTICLE sets out to show the reality and meaning of faith in Christ *from* the standpoint of oppression, as requested. So it makes no direct attempt at dogmatic Christological formulations, nor at working out the question of what is meant by Jesus' sonship in fundamental theological terms. Without denying the importance of either, it concentrates on the relationship between faith in Jesus and oppression: a relationship which can still, indirectly but effectively, shed light on both basic questions.

Oppression is not just one of many hermeneutical situations from which to approach faith in the Son of God, but the situation that is *in fact* the most apt for the Third World today, and *by right* the one that appears throughout Scripture, for understanding the message of salvation. Any Christian theology that is biblical and therefore historical, has to take the most serious account of the signs of the times in its reflections; and even when these are many, one recurs throughout history: 'This sign is always the people crucified in history, uniting an ever-varying form of crucifixion with its continued existence. This crucified people is the historical continuation of the servant of Yahweh, who is stripped of everything by the sin of the world, even of his life, and above all of his life.'[1]

1. THE SERVANT OF YAHWEH AND THE CRUCIFIED PEOPLE

It would be an historical and theological error to understand oppression only '*doloristically*' as an exaltation of sorrow and an apotheosis of suffering, or *ascetically* as the ideal setting for the practice of virtue. If oppression has become a sign of the times, and if it is to be recognised as such and experienced in a Christian fashion, it is because it has been accompanied by the hope and practice of liberation, which are central to the Christian faith.[2]

But it is equally fatal to faith, as well as offensive to the oppressed, to concentrate on liberation without going deeply into the abyss of oppression, which, far from disappearing, is increasing to the limits of horror in countries such as El Salvador and Guatemala. This is repeating the perennial temptation facing Christian faith and theology to exalt the risen Christ without appreciating the horrors of the cross on the historical level.

(*a*) From the standpoint of oppression, faith in the Son of God comes about in the first instance through the *likeness* that exists between a crucified people and the Son of God who took on the condition of a slave. Faith in the *uios Theou* is mediated above all through his resemblance to the *pais Theou* spoken of in the NT (see Matt. 12:13; Acts 3:13, 26; 4:27, 30), which translated the *ebed Jahvé*, as Isaiah presents him in the songs of the servant.

Theologically, this resemblance cannot be turned into pure identity, and we need to analyse what precisely the resemblance consists of. There is the familiar exegetical problem of whether the servant of Yahweh refers to an individual, a group—the remnant of Israel—or the whole collectivity of the people. But whatever the latest position on these details, the fact that there is a resemblance cannot be denied, as Mgr. Romero expressed it on a pastoral level: 'In Christ we meet the type of the liberator, the man who is so identified with the people that biblical exegetes can no longer distinguish whether the Servant of Yahweh proclaimed by Isaiah is the suffering people or Christ come to redeem us.'[3] The real nature of this *pais Theou*, who by virtue of being this is *the* Son of God and not just any son of any god, can be deduced from Isaiah's description of him. His basic features are these:

(*i*) The servant's mission is saving, a salvation that is expressed in the liberating line of the Old Testament, as 'Faithfully he brings true justice;/he will neither waver, nor be crushed/until true justice is established on earth' (42:3-4). He is presented in a partisan and polemical spirit, since his mission is directed to the oppressed and is to 'open the eyes of the blind,/to free captives from prison,/and those who live in darkness from the dungeon' (42:7).

(*ii*) The servant is chosen, but his election is not only a manifestation of the sovereign freedom of God, which could be arbitrary, but of a scandalous will on God's part, since he is chosen to save 'him whose life is despised, whom the nations loathe,/. . . the slave of despots' (49:7); the chosen one is nothing in the eyes of the world and still more one who is crushed by the powers of the world. And inversely, the servant trusts in this scandalous God, who chooses scandalously, that 'all the while my cause was with Yahweh,/my reward with my God' (49:4).

(*iii*) The servant in the end appears destroyed by men in history, so that he 'seemed no longer human' (52:14 f.; 53:2 f.), abandoned, with no one to come to his defence or plead his cause (53:8). He is even shown as sharing the lot of sinners, being taken for one of them (53:12), being given a tomb with the wicked (53:9), regarded as an outcast, someone punished, struck down by God (53:4).

(*iv*) This destiny was produced by the sins of mankind. The servant dies for these sins and these sins lead him to death. The historical correlation between sin and producing death is affirmed, elevated to a universal drama (53:5, 8, 12).

(*v*) The great paradox and scandal is that in the death that comes about through bearing the sins of many, there is salvation (53:5, 11). And it is suggested, inversely, that salvation comes about *only* by his bearing these sins.

(*vi*) This servant has triumphed through being a servant (53:10-12). His condition of a slave not only produces salvation for others, but exaltation for himself. In the New Testament, it is claimed that this *pais Theou* is the *Kyrios*, the Lord (Phil. 2:8-11); that he is the Son of God, constituted as Son precisely through obedience, but without forgetting that 'this obedience is for the servant specifically translated into taking upon himself the sins of mankind'.[4]

(*b*) These characteristics of the servant of Yahweh, of the crucified Son of God, have been rediscovered in Latin America not through mere exegetical curiosity, not just through apologetic concern to support a soteriological theory which affirms that—at the end of the day—life comes out of death. This would be to mock those who are truly oppressed, an *a priori* dialectical, but not necessarily Christian, theodicy. If *these* characteristics of the Son of God have been rediscovered, it is because they have common ground, affinity, likeness with the situation there.

It is not easy to decide exactly how a crucified people can today be the continuation of the servant of Yahweh, a question which Ignacio Ellacuria has examined in depth.[5] But there is no doubt that many people in Latin America reproduce one or more of his characteristics, either simultaneously or complementarily. These are peoples who no longer appear human, as Puebla reminded us, who are deprived of all justice, their basic rights violated, and in particular their right to life threatened by sudden arrest, torture, assassination and mass murder. They are also peoples who, like the servant, try to bring right and justice, who struggle for liberation, this being understood not only as liberation of the group that fights for it, but liberation of the whole people of the poor. Then they are peoples who not only express oppression in the facts of their own existence, but who are actively repressed and persecuted when, like the servant, they try to establish right and justice. Finally, they are peoples who know that they have been chosen as a vehicle of salvation and who interpret their own oppression and repression as the road to liberation. Taken as a whole, many peoples in Latin America are the expression and product of the historical sin of mankind; they bear this sin, struggle against it, while the power of historical sin is turned against them, bringing them death.

Exactly who constitutes this crucified people and how exactly they reproduce the features of the servant is something that needs further analysis. But, structurally speaking, there can be no doubt that this people is not to be found among the powerful of the earth, not in the wealthy nations; nor can it simply be said to be found in the Church, except in that Church that has been persecuted for its option for the poor and has shared the fate of the crucified people. This people is made up of the poor majorities who die slowly as a result of oppression and structural injustice, or quickly as a result of repression by the forces of institutionalised violence. Taken as a whole, this people is what 'makes up all that still has to be undergone by Christ' (Col. 1:24). So Mgr. Romero could say, with pastoral foresight, in his Corpus Christi address: 'It is most opportune to pay homage to the Body and Blood of the Son of Man while there are so many outrages to his body and blood among us. I should like to join this homage of our faith to the presence of the Body and Blood of Christ, which we have shed, with all the blood shed, and the corpses piled up, here in our own land and throughout the world.'[6]

(*c*) This first but basic resemblance to the servant makes something basic possible for faith in the Son of God. A people that suffers in this way, that is so disfigured, tortured and murdered, has no need of processes of demythologisation or sophisticated hermeneutics to find in this Son, in the first place, a close brother. Through looking at Christ crucified, they come to know themselves better, and through looking at themselves, they come to know Christ crucified better. What the Letter to the Hebrews states then becomes a spontaneous reality: 'For the one who sanctifies, and the ones who are sanctified, are of the same stock; that is why he openly calls them "*brothers*" ' (2:11). It may seem that being able to call Christ 'brother' does not mean a great advance in faith; but it is still an advance compared to those—the rich in material goods, those who exercise an authority which is not one of service, whose science is their god—who cannot openly call Christ 'brother'.

2. FOLLOWING CHRIST AND BECOMING 'SONS'

This first likeness to the servant produces an advance in faith to the extent that a crucified people conceives and lives its condition, its cause and its destiny as following Jesus. This is the form of believing in the Son of God from oppression taken in praxis, but it is a real belief. The degree to which faith really comes about in this way cannot, in the final analysis, be quantified, since this is part of the mystery of man before God. But speaking about following Jesus means speaking about the basic structure of a real act of faith and a historical principle of verifying this faith.

(a) The first element of this following is incarnation. This is clear on the basis of Christ's taking flesh. But it is not a question of taking any sort of flesh, but of taking on all that is weak and little in the flesh of history; we are dealing with a consciously partisan incarnation. To become incarnate in this way is to place oneself in the correct position for enabling oneself, through its very reality, to go on making a Christian choice when faced with the alternatives that face everyone in the course of life: riches or poverty, vainglory or humiliation, power or service.

A crucified people is already materially in this incarnation, and only needs to adopt it consciously in faith—whatever the degree of consciousness involved on the psychological level. Those who sociologically do not belong to this crucified people have to achieve this through consciously lowering themselves, integrating themselves in the people in various ways, making common cause with the crucified people, taking on their struggle and their destiny. This type of partisan incarnation is already an expression of faith in Christ.

(b) The second element in this following is the practice of liberation, understood as the liberation brought by Jesus, as announcement of the kingdom of God to the poor and the various forms of service to make this announcement become reality. By its own historical condition, a crucified people already carries out various aspects of Jesus' service to the kingdom *in actu*. Its own existence, once it is aware of it, becomes a word which unmasks false gods—political and economic—in whose name oppression is ideologically justified. But beyond this, its practice formally becomes following by maintaining two essential points.

The first is the maintaining of the hope, not merely the announcement, of the coming of the kingdom. Faced with the delays and rejections of the kingdom in history, maintaining faith in its coming is already a sign of indestructible hope in the God of the kingdom: a hope which becomes the driving force of the practice of liberation. The second is maintaining love as the formal motivation behind the practice of liberation. Latin American theology has analysed at length[7] the fact that love needs historical mediations; this fact is also a requirement of faith in the Holy Spirit, which renews the face of the earth. What needs saying here is that in its just struggle to move from *infra-existence* to *existence*, the crucified people should maintain its *pro-existence*, that the element of salvation of 'the other' should not be lost sight of in the struggle for one's own liberation. This 'other' is in the first place the totality of the world of the oppressed, for whose liberation the individual or group involved in the process of liberation should fight; but it is also the oppressor, whose salvation is also sought in the process of liberation. Although this process generates serious conflicts, its basic dynamism comes from love of other people, not from hatred or vengeance.

(c) The third element is Jesus' aim, set out programatically in the beatitudes, particularly the version in Luke, which shows them concerned with material conditions of poverty, hunger and affliction. But they are also concerned with the spirit in which these material realities should be lived and this is what sets the aim of those who follow Jesus. This spirit is Utopian on account of the historical difficulty of achieving it fully and the difficulty of combining it with other demands of the following of Jesus, such as clear denunciation and unmasking, with the conflictivity and antagonisms they generate, and the effectiveness that must be sought in the process of liberation. But it is a spirit that must always be sought as it is Jesus' will, and because, furthermore, it lends its own efficacy to the practice of historical liberation.[8]

This means that the followers of Jesus must always keep a spirit of mercy in their hearts in the midst of the struggle necessary to achieve justice; they must keep a clear eye open to God's truth: he does not trivialise the struggles of the oppressed by reducing them all to equal value, but judges them by what they can produce; they must work for peace, make the ideal of peace an ingredient in the struggle for justice, even though this struggle, however justly and even nobly undertaken, always involves some degree of violence, which in extreme cases can even include legitimate armed insurrection.[9] They must above all be ready to face persecution, to bear themselves with fortitude in persecution, even to the point of giving their lives, a sign of the greatest love that man can have, and proof that following Jesus is really pro-existence.

(d) A crucified people resembles Jesus by the mere fact of what it is, and is loved preferentially by God because of what it is. But if it changes its outward condition into following Jesus, then it knows him 'from within' and grasps him not only as close brother, but as elder brother, as the first-born. Then what Paul said becomes a historical reality: 'They are the ones he chose specially long ago and intended to become true images of his Son, so that his Son might be the eldest of many brothers' (Rom. 8:29). The reality of the act of faith in Christ comes about in this reproducing of his features, in this becoming sons in the Son.

3. FAITH IN THE SON OF GOD

I have no doubt that in Latin America today this following of Jesus, and therefore this faith in Christ, exists in large measure. I should like to end with a necessarily brief reflection on what the foregoing means in terms of the reality of a Christ believed in under the title of Son of God.

(a) In my view, the very existence of a crucified people brings out, and in its most radical form, a seeking for ultimate reality and for the reality of the divine. We would be misunderstanding the whole question if we were to think that basically theological reflections merely served to justify political and socio-economic choices. They certainly do this, and it is important that they should do so in order to show that faith works in history. But the inverse proposition is equally true. The very historical reality of a crucified people is clamouring for God, even before this clamour is consciously expressed. If anywhere, it is here that the 'problem' of God is posed. Faced with the alternatives of life or death, liberation or oppression, salvation or condemnation, grace or sin, the transcendent quest for God appears in historical form.

A crucified people that also persists in following Jesus has already given a Christian answer to the problem, by transforming it into a 'mystery'. If it holds firm to its process of liberation, if it stands firm in hope, if it believes that the kingdom of God is coming, and, on the other hand, believes it has to bear the sin of the world and that this bearing sin is saving, then it is saying, wordlessly, something extremely important about God, just as Pauline theology did in its day. It is saying that God is salvation, that he raises Jesus, and 'calls into being what does not exist' (Rom. 4:18). At the same time, the cross is a portent of God: 'God's foolishness is wider than human wisdom, and God's weakness is stronger than human strength' (1 Cor. 1:25). This is the mystery of God and the final word on reality. God draws history to himself, submerging himself in the horrors of that history. A crucified people that at one and the same time upholds the liberator God of the Exodus and the God of the cross, is stating that it believes in God and what it means by that God in whom it believes.

(b) This shows what is meant by the 'God' of whom Jesus is 'the Son'. If we believe in Jesus as the Son it is because in him the truth and love of the mystery of God have been shown in an unrepeatable form; and been shown in a way that is totally convincing to a crucified people, who have no problem in accepting Jesus' unrepeatable relationship with God, so that they can confess him to be in truth the Son of God.

The formulation 'Son'—a human word and therefore never totally adequate for describing Jesus—is a good vehicle for expressing the obedience, trust and faithfulness to God that Jesus showed in his life on earth; it also describes well the experience a crucified people has of God: trust in liberation, obedience to the service of liberation, faithfulness in this service, whatever the consequences. What is implied in the metaphor of 'Son' can be accepted from the reality of being Jesus' 'brother'.

Formulations of belief in Christ are important, but of secondary importance compared to what is really believed. In Latin America he is called *the* Liberator. Theologians can and must examine these formulations to show their equivalence with those of the New Testament and the *magisterium*. But what matters is how this faith is expressed in practice. As Karl Rahner has recently said, where Jesus 'in fact works on a specific person so decisively that the person is inspired to give himself unconditionally in life and death to Jesus and therefore decides to believe in the God of Jesus',[10] then that person really and fully believes in Jesus as the Son of God.

This is really happening for many Christians who are giving themselves in life and death to Jesus, who believe in him and in the God he called Father. What I have tried to show here is that this happens *from within* oppression, and, historically, *because* oppression has been taken on in a consciously Christian manner.

Translated by Paul Burns

Notes

    1. I. Ellacuria 'Discernir "el signo" de los tiempos' *Diakonía* 17 (April 1981) 58.
    2. Medellín was careful to link the 'injustice that cries out to heaven' (*Justice*, 1) with the 'desire for total emancipation, for liberation from every form of slavery, for personal maturation and collective integration' (*Intro.*, 4). Both things taken together constitute the signs of the times.
    3. Homily of 21 October 1979, in J. Sobrino *et al. La voz de los sin voz* (San Salvador 1980) p. 366.
    4. Ch. Duquoc *Christologie* (Paris 1973) p. 143.
    5. 'El pueblo crucificado' in Various *Cruz y Resurrección* (Mexico 1978); 'Las bienaventuranzas como carta fundamental de la Iglesia de los pobres' in Various *Iglesia de los pobres y organizaciones populares* (San Salvador 1979) pp. 105-118; 'El verdadero pueblo de Dios', shortly to appear in *Diakonía*.
    6. Homily of 21 June 1979, in the work cited in note 3 p. 337.
    7. See J. Sobrino 'Following Jesus as Discernment' in *Concilium* 9 (1978) 14.
    8. Mgr. Romero was an outstanding example of how to combine the practice of effective liberation with the spirit of the beatitudes. See J. Sobrino 'La Iglesia en el actual proceso del pais' in *ECA* 372/3 (1979) 918-920; 'Mons. Romero y la Iglesia salvadoreña, un año después' in *ibid*. 389 (1981) 148-150.
    9. See Mgr. Romero's third and fourth pastoral letters in *La voz de los sin voz* pp. 113-119, 156-159; 'Compromiso cristiano para una Nicaragua nueva', Pastoral letter of the Nicaraguan bishops, 17 November 1979.
    10. *¿Que debemos creer todavía?* (Santander 1980) p. 106.

PART II

The Biblical, Liturgical and Conciliar Foundations of the Term 'Jesus, Son of God'

Herbert Haag

'Son of God' in the Language and Thinking of the Old Testament

1. THE PHAROAH AS 'TRUE GOD AND TRUE MAN'

THE TITLE 'son of God' is a dominant one in the writings of the New Testament, and even more so in the dogma of the Church. This title does not have its original roots in the Old Testament. We find it first of all in the ancient East, especially Egypt. Here it was the Pharoah who bore the title of 'son of (the sun) God'.[1] He was both true God and true man. His double nature was described in mythical terms by saying that he was the son of an earthly—and virgin—mother and a divine father. The father God was initially the sun god, Re. In the course of the twentieth century before Christ, however, the national god Amun took Re's place. It was Amun who begot the king on the virgin. As the son of God, the king was 'of one body with the father'—that is to say, the same in essence. However, this divine sonship was proclaimed only from the day when the king ascended the throne. Up to then he was simply the son of the reigning king and the king's wife. His ascent of the throne showed him to be the one chosen by heaven; and he was thereby designated son of God (see Rom. 1:4). The fact that the Pharoah had older brothers and sisters was not felt to be any contradiction of this conception.

The Egyptian myth about the physical divine sonship of the king was unique in the ancient world. In Mesopotamia especially we find no trace of it at all. It is true that the Sumerians occasionally called their king the son of God. But this was evidently intended to be understood in a wider sense, as an indication that he belonged to the realm of the divine generally; this is already suggested by the fact that the king could call himself the son of several gods simultaneously. In Semitic cuneiform literature the title has faded completely.

2. THE DAVIDIC KING AS 'SON OF GOD'

In view of Israel's close ties with Egypt—especially after the monarchy was consolidated in the empire of David and Solomon—it would in fact be surprising if the Egyptian idea about the divine sonship of the king had failed to spread to Israel. And the title 'son of God' is applied to the dynasty of David and its current representative in several passages in the Old Testament.

2.1. The basic text is *the Nathan prophecy* in 2 Samuel 7. It must be said, however, that in the form in which it has come down to us this chapter is not a homogeneous whole. It has been subjected to a considerable number of revisions. There is no doubt that the contrast between 'Would you build me a house?' (v. 5b) and 'Yahweh will make you a house' (v. 11b) was part of the passage in its earliest form. Here the word 'house' is meant both literally and in a transferred sense, for the dynasty. In verses 12 and 14-16 the promise of a house to be given to David is developed further: the house that Yahweh is going to build for David is his 'seed'—his descendants. Yahweh will 'raise up' his 'offspring' and 'establish' his kingdom, so that David's throne will 'be made sure for ever'. But this 'house' is not only subject to grace. It is open to judgment too. The underlying presumption is that it is going to transgress and that Yahweh will then punish it as a father punishes his son—though this does not mean that Yahweh will withdraw his love. The saying 'I will be to him his father, and he shall be my son' refers to this fatherly love and severity. Moreover it does not apply to the individual king. It is meant for the dynasty as a whole. Verse 13, on the other hand, with its 'He shall build a house for my name' is in fact a clear reference to Solomon. But this verse must be viewed as a later addition.

2.2. *Psalm 89* is clearly a development of the theology underlying 2 Samuel 7. The Davidic dynasty is in its final throes, if it is not already dead; and so the petitioner compares the glorious promises of the past with the desolate present:

Of old thou didst speak in a vision to thy faithful one, and say: . . .
I have found David, my servant;
with my holy oil I have anointed him; . . .
He shall cry to me, 'Thou art my Father,
my God, and the Rock of my salvation'.
And I will make him the first-born,
the highest of the kings of the earth   (vv. 19, 20, 26 f.).

Here, too, the name 'David' stands for the whole Davidic dynasty; for the promise quoted was not given to David as an individual, but to his 'seed'. The house of David is certainly not called Yahweh's 'son'. But nevertheless a unique father-son relationship between the two is asserted. Yahweh lets David call upon him as 'father'; and he himself designates 'David' as his 'first-born son'—indeed he is to be the 'highest' among all the kings of the earth. Here we find ourselves in the atmosphere of Psalm 72:11. The vista is wide and far-ranging. It reaches out to the great empires of the world, the glories of the Babylonian and (especially) the Persian courts. But even compared with the emperor himself David is the 'first-born son'—a term applied to Israel in Exodus 4:22 and to Ephraim in Jeremiah 31:9. He is indeed the highest of all, the *Elyon*, a title which is applied to a human being in this single passage alone. This moves the monarchy into unique proximity to God. For David does not mean so much the historical king; it is the future David that is in the writer's mind. While the Davidic dynasty lies prostrate, the people watch longingly for the David of the era of salvation to come.

2.3. *Psalm 2* is undoubtedly based on an ancient coronation ritual. This is the case whether it is pre-exilic or whether it is an expression of hope for the messianic king and belongs to the period following the exile. Verse 6 points unequivocally to the enthronement: 'I have set my king on Zion, my holy hill.' But then Yahweh's resolve, 'You are my son, today I have begotten you' (v. 7) cannot be interpreted as meaning engendering in the physical sense (and indeed there was no place for any such notion in the Yahweh religion). The formula 'today I have begotten you' was evidently part of the Israelite coronation ritual. Through his enthronement the king *became* the son of God. The legal and historical background for this idea is not adoption, which was unknown in

Israel; it was the practice whereby a father could recognise as his own the children born to a slave. According to the Babylonian law of Hammurabi, the formula used for this was: 'You are my children' (§ 170 f. See Gen. 30:1-13). In this way, in Israel as in Egypt, the king was designated 'son of God' through the act of ascending the throne (see Rom. 1:4). Israelite practice differed from the Egyptian model, however, in that the divine engendering was not projected back to the beginning of the king's lifetime. Consequently a woman is never mentioned in connection with the divine sonship of the Israelite king. The event took place solely between God and the king, and it was purely emblematic. Israel had no intention of attributing a divine 'nature' to the king; this is also made sufficiently clear by the ruthless denunciation of the king's sins.

2.4. Two other passages deserve our attention here. In *Psalm 110* we are also face to face with a coronation ritual. But this one contains such archaic elements that we are forced to assume that it goes back to a Canaanite model. The invitation 'Sit at my right hand' (v. 1) presupposes the custom that was widespread in the ancient East, whereby at his enthronement the king sat at the right hand of the god's image. This was a ritual that was impossible in Israel, with its renunciation of images. In verse 3 we are told about the king who has been enthroned on Zion (I am translating literally):

In holy glory from the womb of the dawn
is for you the dew of your youth (or: your youthful manliness).

The context as a whole suggests that this is a reference to the divine engendering of the king, which took place 'in holy glory' and was 'from the womb of the dawn'. In Ugarite mythology we find a divine couple, Shachar and Shalim, who personify the sunrise and the sunset. Now we are in Jerusalem, whose name undoubtedly contains the divine name Shalim; while in the psalm we meet with Shachar, the sunrise. In ancient Semitic mythology, dew is thought of as being the seed or sperm of the weather god, with which he moistens the earth. So what the psalm originally said was that the dew (= seed) of the god Shalim had engendered the king from the womb of Shachar the dawn. It is obvious that a statement of this kind would have scandalised Yahweh worshippers. The obscurity of the text as it has come down to us (it has more hints than clear statements) is therefore probably due to a deliberate disguising of the tenor of the Canaanite model when it was taken over into an Israelite and Yahwistic context. The vagueness is probably deliberate. On the other hand, we find confirmation here, as in Psalm 2, for the supposition that the enthronement was compared with a divine begetting.

2.5. The last significant passage is the proclamation of salvation in *Isaiah 9:6 f.* (though it is improbable that the saying derives from Isaiah himself):

To us a child is born, to us a son is given;
and the government will be upon his shoulder,
and the name he will be given will be Wonderful Counsellor, Divine Hero,
Everlasting Father, Prince of Peace.

Here the king's birth and his enthronement are seen together in a single vista. The parallelism between 'son' and 'child' points to an entirely human birth. But at his enthronement the king receives among other titles the name of '*ēl qibbōr*, 'divine hero'. It must be remembered, however, that in the Old Testament the word 'divine' often simply means 'mighty'. (What the German Bible and the Bible de Jérusalem translate as 'the cedars of God' in Psalm 80.10 rightly appear in English as 'the mighty cedars'.) So the 'divine hero' is nothing more than the 'mighty hero'. It was in no way Israel's intention to attribute divinity to the ruler of the era of salvation to come.

2.6. We must look once more at the Nathan prophecy, this time in the version we find in the Chronicler's history. At first sight the account in 1 Chronicles 17 seems identical with the one given in 2 Samuel 7. But in fact the Chronicler, as he often does, has made some small but significant changes, in line with his own theology. Instead of 'I will raise up your offspring after you, who shall come forth from your body' (2 Sam. 7:12), he says: 'I will raise up your offspring after you, one of your own sons' (v. 11). This makes the promise apply to an individual, instead of to the collective 'seed', or descendants. And whereas the relationship between father and son in 2 Samuel 7 is seen pre-eminently in the fact that the son is punished when he transgresses, Chronicles does not envisage the possibility that the king will err:

> I will be his father, and he shall be my son; I will not take my steadfast love from him, as I took it from him who was before you (v. 13).

In the period when the Chronicler was writing (about 300 B.C.) Israel was without a king; and the writer's hope was directed towards a ruler belonging to the Davidic line who would be without any human weaknesses. If we agree with the messianic interpretation of the statement, this is the first passage in the Scriptures—and, moreover, the only passage in the whole body of pre-Christian Jewish writings—in which the Messiah is formally called 'the son of God' (for Qumran see below). But even this son of God is entirely a son of David. The divine sonship is restricted to the context of his election and to the intimacy of the relation.

3. SONS OF GOD AT THE HEAVENLY COURT

Up to now the results of our investigations have been somewhat meagre. It is only twice, in Psalm 2:7 and 1 Chronicles 17:13, that the king as individual is called 'son of God'. But these two passages are all the more noteworthy because this title—with a single exception, which we shall be looking at presently—is never otherwise attributed to an individual at all in the Old Testament. At the same time, we must remember that the word 'son' (*ben*) is used in the Old Testament for a variety of relationships. It was not merely the name given to man's descendant in the physical sense. It also meant belonging to a particular people, town, professional group or region. The men belonging to the people of Israel are 'the sons of Israel'; the inhabitants of Jerusalem are 'the sons of Jerusalem' (Isa. 51:18 and frequently elsewhere); arrows are 'the sons of the bow' (Job 41:28) or 'the sons of the quiver' (Lam. 3:13); 'the sons of the prophets' are the members of the prophets' brotherhoods or guilds (1 Kings 20:35 and frequently elsewhere); a 'son of the ointment mixer' (Neh. 3:8) is a member of the guild of apothecaries. In the same way the term 'sons of God' or 'sons of the gods' in the Old Testament means beings belonging to the region of the gods or the heavenly world. Israel came to terms with the motley Canaanite pantheon, not merely by identifying its highest God, El, with Yahweh, and by eliminating the other gods. These were also disempowered and degraded to the rank of 'sons of God'—that is to say, beings who were subordinate to Yahweh and formed his royal household. This applies both to the 'sons of the gods' who cannot exist on a level with Yahweh and have to pay homage to him (Ps. 89:6; 29:1) and to the 'sons of the Most High' whom Yahweh judges (Ps. 82:6), as well as to the 'sons of the Gods' who took the daughters of men as wives (Gen. 6:2, 4), and to those who in the Prologue to the Book of Job (chapter 1) appear before Yahweh in order to receive his instructions (1:6; 2:1) and who rejoiced over the works of God on the very morning of creation (Job 38:7). The fact that in the 'frame' story of the Book of Job even Satan is one of the sons of God shows how widely the title was applied in Israel, even in post-exilic times.

4. ISRAEL AS THE SON OF GOD

Above all, however, it is the intimate relationship between Yahweh and Israel which is depicted as the relationship between father and son. Yahweh calls Israel 'my son' (Exod. 4:23; Hos. 11:1) and 'my first-born son' (Exod. 4:22; Jer. 31:9); he calls the Israelites 'my sons' (Isa. 45:11 A.V.) and 'my sons and daughters' (Isa. 43:6); they are called 'sons' (Isa. 63:8), 'his sons' (Deut. 32:5, in the Hebrew) and 'his sons and daughters' (Deut. 32:19). Yahweh is correspondingly addressed as 'father'. This funds expression particularly in the, roughly, forty personal names which include the element 'father' ('āb). Abram is an example ('my father is high, elevated'); so is Abner ('my father is a light'), and above all Abiel ('my father is El') and Abijahu ('my father is Yahweh'). These names (some of which are very old) probably expressed, at least originally, not so much a relationship enjoyed by the individual owner of the name, as the relationship of his whole kindred or clan to the tribal god. In this context the tribe is thought of as being engendered by the tribal god. This is the reason why it knows that it owes a duty to this god alone; but that it can equally expect from him guidance and protection. In the Old Testament too the fatherhood of Yahweh is based on the fact of creation. This is brought out in the Song of Moses (Deut. 32):

Is he not your father, who created you,
Is it not he who made you and established you? (v. 6)

and in Trito-Isaiah:

Yet, O Yahweh, thou art our Father;
we are the clay, and thou art our potter;
we are all the work of thy hand   (Isa. 64:8; see 45:9-11).

The father-son relationship between Yahweh and Israel is especially stressed when it is a matter of Yahweh's electing and continually disappointed love. Hosea feels that Yahweh's adoption of Israel as son is something profoundly tragic:

When Israel was a child, I loved him,
and out of Egypt I called my son.
The more I called them,
the more they went from me. . . .
Yet it was I who taught Ephraim to walk,
I took them up in my arms (Hos. 11:1-3).

5. THE DEVOUT AS THE SONS OF GOD

The king as son of God, the angels as sons of God, Israel as son of God—is this title applied to 'ordinary' people as well in the Old Testament? The earlier texts only talk in the plural about 'sons of the living God' (Hos. 1:10), 'sons of Yahweh' (Deut. 14:1) or simply 'sons' (Isa. 1:2; 30:1—in the Hebrews; Jer. 3:22). In the later literature this changes. It is true that there, too, we only hear of 'daughters of God' in the collective plural (Wis. 9:7; see 2 Cor. 6:18). On the other hand the Book of Wisdom talks at some length about the devout *individual* as son of God. Liberal Jews who cherish the Epicurean philosophy of their Hellenistic environment mock at faithfulness to the law:

> But let us lie in wait for the righteous man,
> Because he is of disservice to us.
> The latter end of the righteous he calleth happy;
> And he vaunteth that God is his father.
> Let us see if his words be true,
> And let us try what shall befall in the ending of his life.
> For if the righteous man is God's son, he will uphold him,
> And he will deliver him out of the hand of his adversaries   (Wis. 2:12, 16-18).

And Jesus Sirach admonishes his pupil:

> Be as a father to orphans . . .
> Then God will call thee 'son'   (Ecclus. 4:10).

This suggests that among Hellenistic Jews the devout man claimed the title of son of God for himself without scruple. The Palestinian Jews were much more reticent in this respect. In the Hebrew writings of Qumran, the designation 'son of God' is found only once, in a quotation from 2 Sam. 7:10-14 (4 QFlor I, 10-13). More important is the fragment of an Aramaean text belonging to the last thirty years or so of the first century B.C. (4Q 246). The text is hard to interpret and may perhaps have an apocalyptic reference. Here a ruler—probably a worldy one—is called 'son of God' and 'son of the Highest'.[2] It is unlikely that the ruler is thought of as a messianic figure, however. Up to now we have no reliable evidence at all to suggest that the title 'son of God' was given a messianic application among Palestinian Jews at the time of Jesus.

Summing up it may be said that in the Old Testament and in early Judaism the title 'son of God' signifies creatureliness, election and intimacy. It has no messianic connotation, and it is certainly not intended to signify divinity.[3]

Translated by Margaret Kohl

Notes

1. E. Brunner-Traut 'Pharaoh und Jesus als Söhne Gottes' *Antaios* 2 (1961) 266-284 = *Gelebte Mythen* (Wiesbaden 1981) pp. 34-54; H. Brunner *Die Geburt des Gottkönigs* (Wiesbaden 1964).

2. J. A. Fitzmyer *A Wandering Aramaean* (Ann Arbor 1979) pp. 90-94 and 102-107.

3. For the most important literature on the subject, see the following: G. Fohrer, E Schweizer & E. Lohse *Theol. Wörterbuch zum NT* VIII pp. 340-363; H. Haag *Theol. Wörterbuch zum AT* I pp. 670-682; J. de Fraine *L'Aspect religieux de la royauté israélite* (Rome 1954); G. Cooke 'The Israelite King as Son of God' *Zeitschrift f. d. alttest. Wissenschaft* 73 (1961) 202-225 and 'The Sons of (the) God(s)' *Zeitschrift f. d. alttest. Wissenschaft* (76) 22-47; W. Schlisske *Gottessöhne und Gottessohn im Alten Testament* (Stuttgart 1973); P. A. H. de Boer 'The Son of God in the Old Testament' *Oudtest. Stud* 18 (1973) 188-207; J. L. Cunchillos *Cuando los angeles eran dioses* (Salamanca 1976).

Bas van Iersel

'Son of God' in the New Testament

THERE IS every reason to begin this article where the one by H. Haag ends. When Christians of the first generation call Jesus 'Son of God', this is very recognisably linked with the Old Testament roots of this way of speaking. Of all the Old Testament places where an individual person is called by this name, by far most are incorporated in the New Testament, often with explicit reference, and in some cases—as in Ps. 2:7 and 110:1—even in various places in different writings. It is desirable, however, to draw explicit attention to some points of the above-mentioned article, as they are of uncommon importance for the understanding of the New Testament.

First of all, the word 'son' (*ben*) in biblical Hebrew was used much more widely than in modern languages. Thus the teacher of wisdom in Proverbs addresses himself more than twenty times to his hearer/reader with 'my son' (*beni*). The same was the case with the title 'father'. The phenomenon is also found in modern languages (father, père, padre); but in these cases the use is limited to very specific instances. In Hebrew every man of advanced years could be addressed as 'father' if one wished to honour him. This is important, because it shows that in the social surroundings where Christians called Jesus for the first time 'Son of God', the words 'father' and 'son' had to do much less exclusively with blood-relationship and descent than is the case in modern languages. In the New Testament this holds good also for the Greek, for example where persons are addressed as 'child' (*teknon*) or 'little children' (*teknia*) and venerable persons as 'father' (Matt. 23:9-10). In such a social setting the title 'Son of God' does not necessarily express a relationship of descent, but could just as well signify something like 'closely united to . . .' or 'belonging to God'.

A second point concerns the title 'Son of God' as given to the king from the house of David and to the expected messianic king. That God according to Old Testament ideas considered this king his son is beyond doubt. But it should be mentioned that so far nowhere in the Old Testament or in inter-testamental literature has the combination 'Son of God' (*ben elohim* or *ben JHWH*) been found to describe this figure. Neither is it found in the collection of messianic quotations of the Qumran documents, which do quote 2 Sam. 7:10-14 but do not mention the title 'Son of God'. The only place where so far it has been found is in the Aramaic fragment mentioned by H. Haag, which speaks of 'the Son of God' (*bereh di el*) and 'Son of the Most High' (*bar 'eljon*). But this, too, has not been able to affect the conclusion drawn from the earlier-known texts: as a sort of regular or generally accepted title for the Messiah, 'Son of God' does not occur in pre-Christian literature. This must have consequences for the origin of the title as applied to Jesus. For in that case one cannot simply say that the first generation of Christians, calling Jesus 'Son of God', did no more than transfer to him an existing title belonging to the expected Messiah.

Finally a third point which is not altogether unimportant. In the Old Testament the special bond with God is expressed by the word 'son' in the case of four categories of persons: members of the heavenly court, the people of Israel, their king, and the persecuted just. But in the Old Testament these four have remained juxtaposed without being linked together. This is completely different in the New Testament. For the heavenly court the title no longer occurs, although Luke 20:36 shows that there remains an association between 'sons of God' and angels. Heb. 1-2 even asserts emphatically that it is to Jesus alone and not to angels that this title belongs. However, where in the New Testament Christians are called 'sons of God', this is never done without a clear reference to the one 'Son of God', who is the first-born among many brethren (Rom. 8:29).

Now in starting our investigation and trying to ascertain what this title means in the books of the New Testament we shall indeed have a look at all the different phases, but we shall focus our attention in particular on two questions. The first one concerns the beginning of Jesus' public ministry and the impression this caused among the people to whom he addressed himself. The second concerns the development of the meaning of the title at the time when the New Testament was being completed.

1. THE BEGINNING

When the oldest book of the New Testament—in all probability Paul's first letter to the Christians of Thessalonica, written round the year 50—is committed to paper, Jesus has been dead for almost twenty years. There is no doubt at all that those who believed in him did not remain silent during this period. But this does not take away from the fact that the reconstruction of traditions circulating about him always retains something hypothetical. For that reason it remains a hazardous undertaking to try to look behind the writings of the New Testament. If nevertheless we are going to do so in this article, we will limit ourselves to a few issues on which there exists a high degree of consensus.[1] In doing so we base ourselves on the view that—as was already said above—the opinion according to which the first generation of Christians simply applied to Jesus the messianic title 'Son of God', is untenable as long as it has not been proved that this title was indeed in general use. As the chronological ordering of these pre-existing traditions must necessarily remain a matter for speculation, we will discuss them in the order in which we find them in the New Testament, even if Paul's letters are older than the gospels and probably contain earlier material.

That the first three gospels incorporated a great deal of material from tradition is certain. But often the pre-existing narratives cannot be reconstructed or at most with insufficient certainty. This holds good, for example, for the narrative of Jesus' trial (Mark 14:5-15 par.) which is of the utmost importance for our subject. Of other narratives, for example that of Jesus' glorification (Mark 9:2-8 par.), it is sufficiently certain that they are older than the gospels, but it is hardly possible to ascertain what the word 'son' exactly implied. Which leaves us with the following four narrative texts.

The first is the extremely short account of what happens at Jesus' baptism (Mark 1:9-11 par.). When after the immersion he emerges from the water he sees the heavens split asunder and the Spirit descend upon him, and he hears a voice from heaven saying to him: 'Thou art my beloved son, in Thee I am well pleased.' If we compare this passage with Ez. 1-2, Ps. 2:7 and Isa. 42:1 it appears to have been put together from pre-existing themes and motifs. Only the account of the baptism forms an exception to this. If the narrative originated among the members of a community for whom the thoughts of

Rom. 8:14-17; 1 Cor. 12:13 and Gal. 4:6-7 had already become common property—which is perfectly possible but cannot be proved—the combination, too, of baptism, spirit and sonship would be very obvious. At any rate the narrative shows Jesus towering above all his contemporaries, even above John the Baptist, and to speak and act from the beginning of his public ministry as the messianic king of Ps. 2:7. It is striking that of this verse the second part 'this day have I begotten thee' is not mentioned, whereas Acts 13:33 and Heb. 1:5 do include it. Can something be deducted from this? Perhaps the following: that the narrative wants to take the title 'son' out of the context of consanguinity and descent, or that it considers the narrated events rather as an indication of Jesus as Messiah than as a proclamation or even enthronisation. That he is called God's beloved son shows that like his ancestor David he is a man after God's heart (1 Sam. 13:14; Acts 13:22).

The longer account of Jesus' temptation in the desert (Matt. 4:1-11 par.), too, is certainly of earlier composition than the oldest gospel. The devil starts two of the three temptations with the words: 'If thou art the Son of God. . . .' Taking into account that in Matt. 4:8-9 Jesus is offered power over the world, we may assume that also in the present-day versions the title is given a messianic significance. But the location of Jesus' temptation 'in the desert' makes clear that Jesus is also designated as the epitome of Israel as the chosen Son of God (see especially Deut. 8, of which verse 3 is quoted in Matt. 4:4 par.), who in the desert is given an opportunity to show that he wishes to live in accordance with the will of God.

Mark 12:1-12 par. is a story narrated by the protagonist himself within the greater narrative formed by every gospel. It is highly probable that with the exception of some minor elements the first evangelist drew on accounts already in circulation. It relates, *inter alia*, how the owner of a vineyard, having in vain sent servants to collect the rent, at last sends his son. The fact that he is his only son and that the tenants have already seriously maltreated the servants, makes it a risky undertaking which ends in disaster, the son being killed. No Christian listener or reader will miss the point: the story is about Jesus himself. And the contemporary meanings of the word 'son' are enriched with elements which were not taken from the Old Testament, but from the life story of Jesus and from the way his followers—and probably he himself, too—interpreted it: the son inaugurates the end of time; he is more important than all his predecessors; he is sent by God as the last and most important of a long line; in this undertaking he risks and eventually loses his life. All these, without exception, are concepts which also occur frequently in the writings of Paul and John.

In the narrative of the birth of Jesus and John (Luke 1-2) there is in all probability only little that originates from Luke himself. The various partial narratives which are interrelated want to show first and foremost that Jesus is greater than the baptist. The latter is a 'prophet of the Most High' (1:76), whereas Jesus is called 'Son of the Most High' (1:32), a title which meanwhile has become known to us through the above-mentioned Aramaic Qumran fragment. Here, however, the term certainly has a messianic meaning: God will give him the throne of his father David and he shall reign over the house of Jacob forever (1:32-33). Furthermore the narrative also mentions that he is called 'Son of God' because of his miraculous birth, without the intervention of a man, but through the assistance of the Holy Spirit (v. 35). But it is certain that verse 35 contains an unusually high number of words which are characteristic of Luke's style.[2] This is no definite proof that the original narrative did not contain those words, but it cannot possibly be adduced as evidence that here the pre-Lucan tradition linked the title 'Son of God' with the virgin birth of Jesus, even if the latter event—though without 'Son of God'—occurs in Matt. 1:20.

Not only in the gospels but also in the letters older traditions have been preserved, though normally of a different nature. They are more often than not creeds, liturgical

D

hymns, etc. Two of these are important for our subject. The first one occurs in what is probably Paul's oldest letter, namely the one to the Christians of Thessalonica (A.D. 50). In *1 Thess. 1:9-10* he writes: 'You turned to God from idols, to serve a living and true God, and to wait for his Son from heaven, . . . Jesus, who delivers us from the wrath to come.' It is pretty well generally accepted that this is an implicit quotation of a formula which was in common use in the proclamation of the faith to the heathens. Jesus is not called 'Lord', 'Christ' or 'Messiah', as elsewhere in the letter, but he is related to God as 'his Son', something which occurs only in this passage of the letter. He is given this title in his capacity as the risen Jesus, who after his resurrection is now in heaven, with God, and who at the end of time will appear at the judgment as the saviour of those who believed in him and served the one living God. The 'son' is above all an eschatological figure, who will only become active once more at the end of time when the final judgment begins. In this judgment he exercises the function which according to Mark 14:62 and especially 8:38 is connected with the title 'son of man'.

The second passage is an implicit quotation, found in *Rom. 1:3-4*. In it, as an apposition to 'his (= God's) son', an old formula is inserted, which reads as follows:

'. . . *born of the seed of David* according to the flesh, *who was declared to be the Son of God with power*, according to the Spirit of holiness, *by the resurrection of the dead*; even Jesus Messiah (or Christ) our Lord.'

Of this passage at least the words in italics are of an earlier origin, but possibly also others. 'Son of God' in this context is the title of the messianic king from the house of David. Jesus does not possess this title from birth or from the moment when he appears in public. This dignity was conferred on him at his resurrection from the dead, as is said here. Presumably what is meant here is Jesus' own resurrection, which is then seen as the beginning of the general resurrection (see also Acts 13:33 and Hebr. 1:3-5). In this formula obviously no explicit reference is made to Ps. 2:7 and 2 Sam. 7; but it is nonetheless clear that these passages, in view of the influence they appear to exert elsewhere in the New Testament, have helped to create the formula. Possibly *2 Tim. 2:8* offers an older version, which in that case read simply: 'Jesus Messiah, raised from the dead, from the seed of David.'[3] It is interesting then that the title 'Son of God' was only added to the creed afterwards and that only then it was linked with the resurrection. At any rate we can hold as sufficiently proved that Jesus after his death was proclaimed by his Jewish followers as the risen Messiah from the house of David, to whom the title 'Son of God' belongs by right.

Can we look back even further than the above-mentioned passages allow us to? For they do not take us back further than the period between Jesus' departure and the composition of the earliest New Testament writings. In particular we should ask ourselves if we can use as a source of information what happened *before* that period between Jesus and his followers. Precisely if 'Son of God' was not a current title for the Messiah from the house of David, and certainly when Jesus takes up a more than reticent attitude in respect of the opinion that he is the Messiah, we ask ourselves on what grounds he is later called Son of God. The view that Jesus during his life-time must have pointed to himself as 'the Son of God' (Mark 13:32 par. and Matt. 11:27 par.)[4] has never even remotely found general support, because sufficient doubt persisted about the historical authenticity of the respective utterances. Consequently a direct connection cannot simply be shown to exist.

However, there is an indirect connection. In the first three gospels Jesus often speaks about and to God as his father. This certainly was nothing out of the ordinary. 'Our father in heaven' belongs to the normal Jewish expressions when addressing God in prayer. Precisely the 'in heaven' excludes too great a familiarity, because it underlines the unfathomable distance between those who pray here on earth and him to whom they address themselves. But it is certainly unusual that God is addressed with the simple word 'father'. Of this form of address even the Aramaic word has survived in tradition and it has done so not only in one of the gospels (Mark 14:36) but also in two places in Paul's letters (Rom. 8:15 and Gal. 4:6). There cannot be any doubt at all that here we have a case of authentic use of the language by Jesus which deviated from the general use.[5] The fact that this Aramaic word has penetrated even into Paul's letters shows that it must have made a deep impression. And this is not surprising. Some one who in Jesus' days addressed God like this, was showing unheard of familiarity in his intercourse with God. For even if the word was being used as an honourable title of address, it did not belong to the titles commonly used to address God. Jesus experienced God as his father in a way that had no precedent in the Jewish tradition as far as we can now ascertain. And the memory of this after Jesus' resurrection may have rendered easier the confession that he was and is God's son. Moreover it lends to such a pronouncement an impressive quality of truth.

2. THE FIRST THREE GOSPELS

The gospel according to Mark stands out from the others, not so much by the number of times it calls Jesus 'the Son' and 'the Son of God', but rather by the insertion of these titles in structurally important places of the book. Thus the title occurs right in the beginning, as a kind of caption above the whole book. Even before the story begins the reader knows that it deals with Jesus Christ, the Son of God (1:1), a piece of information reserved for the time being to the reader and to Jesus himself, and as yet not given to the earthly figures occurring in the story. After the name appears in three essential places. First a voice from heaven communicates to Jesus that he is the Son of God (1:11), with the result that Jesus acts as such right from the beginning of the narrative. Halfway through the narrative once more a voice from heaven communicates the same message to Jesus' closest disciples (9:7). And at the end of the book, when Jesus has been executed on the cross and the voice from heaven has remained silent in spite of Jesus' desperate supplications (15:34) a human voice is the first to answer him by taking over the name in a confession (15:39).

For the meaning of the term the first of these three passages is already of great importance. The baptist, himself identified as Elias who has returned (1:2-6; see 6:14-15; 8:28; 9:13; 15:35) and consequently as the last of the prophets and the one who ushers in the end of time, announces that after him one is coming who is stronger than himself. In the narrative the content of his announcement is immediately realised: Jesus comes forward to be baptised, and emerging from the baptismal waters he is given the Spirit. And with Jesus the reader hears a voice from heaven saying: 'Thou art my beloved Son, with thee I am well pleased' (1:9-11). Possessing God's spirit, the son is not only stronger than John the Baptist, but he is also stronger than the evil spirits who have to give way to him (see also 3:27), because they recognise in him the Son of God (3:11; 5:7). Whether also in Mark the voice from heaven points to Jesus as the messianic king, remains to be seen until we penetrate further into the book.

The three disciples who halfway through the book are told by a voice from heaven that Jesus is God's son (9:7), have only just heard from Jesus himself that he will be executed by order of the authorities (8:31) and that he must not refuse this death. Does this mean that we can really understand what it means to be God's son only if besides Jesus' power we have also got to know his vulnerability? Or could it be that Jesus' real power manifests itself only when his life is in danger, because he does not give way when threatened by the powers that be? When we read in 10:32 how intrepidly Jesus leads his frightened disciples to the place of execution, we realise that it is not his vulnerability but his real strength in the face of oppression which the book wants to bring out. Because even where Jesus' powerlessness is shown most clearly, there is evidence of this strength. The first manifestation of this occurs when he stands before his judges, who will see to it that Jesus' liquidation is turned into a judicial murder. The question: 'Art thou the Messiah, the son of the Blessed?' he answers with a wholehearted 'yes', but he adds immediately that one day the roles will be reversed, when he will be sitting at the right hand of power and coming with the clouds of heaven to judge them (14:61-62). The same combination of powerlessness and strength is depicted when Jesus is executed on the cross. Passers-by, scribes and high-priests taunt him with the words: 'He saved others; he cannot save himself. Let the Christ, the King of Israel, come down now from the cross' (15:29-32). The reader has no doubt at all that Jesus has the power to do this. But at the same time he knows that he will not do so. For he did not come to save himself but to save and liberate others. But when Jesus dies, the power of the executed criminal appears to be unbroken: the veil of the temple is torn in two. Then the pagan centurion speaks and utters for the first time a profession of faith: 'Truly this man was the Son of God' (15:39). The voice from heaven has found a hearing also in others than Jesus himself, and received an answer.

But what is really the meaning of the confession that Jesus is the Son of God? It certainly no longer means that Jesus is the messianic king. The book does not contain any indication that the title 'Messiah' expresses adequately who Jesus is. And especially the idea, connected with this, of the kingship of Israel is rejected by the book. Jesus is called 'King of Israel' only by those who execute, torture and scoff him (15:2, 9, 12, 18, 26, 32) and Jesus leaves the responsibility for the title with those who use it (15:2). Even the word 'Messiah' has more to do with misunderstanding (8:29-33) than with faith.[7] Naturally then the question arises, whether other Old Testament places have determined the meaning of the name in Mark. One of these would certainly be Wisdom 2, where the just man who is persecuted is taunted with the fact that he called himself Son of God and maintained that God is his father (Wisd. 2:13, 18-20). Especially the derision of Jesus on the cross reminds us unmistakably of what we read in Wisd. 2. At any rate so unmistakably that Matthew, who in this passage takes over Mark's text virtually without any alterations, complements it with some minor additions which clearly refer to Wisdom (Matt. 27:40, 43).

But this is not all there is to be said. This is clear not only from what was said above about Mark 1:9-11, where Jesus is placed in the line of the prophets and as Son of God is shown to be greater and more powerful than the prophets preceding him. In this respect the parable of the vineyard is important, which was already discussed in the previous paragraph. By adding the word 'beloved' (*agapêtos*) in 12:6 Mark underlined once more that this son is the same as the one in 1:11 and 9:7. In Mark this narrative functions as a mirror-narrative or key-narrative, by being the recapitulation of the narrative as a whole. This key-function holds good also for the name 'Son of God'. By this narrative he is described as a man, sent by God (2:17; 9:37; 10:45), as the last of the prophets, but evidently greater and stronger than his predecessors.

How much greater? So much as to make him equal to God? To be sure, according to Jewish ideas the one who is sent with a message has the same authority as the one who sent him,[8] but this equality is only of a juridical nature (9:37). Not only is there no question of a kind of essential equality between Jesus and God, but Mark clearly reflects a different view. Although God's beloved son is closer to him than any one else, there is tension and dissimilarity between the power (13:39), the knowledge (13:32) and the will (14:36) of the one and the other. Moreover, that the Jesus of Mark does not want to be identified with God, he underlines in 10:18 with the following reaction: 'Why callest thou me good? None is good save one, even God.' He is conscious of acting on God's authority, as is made clear by the question with which he parries the question on whose authority he has driven the merchants and the money-changers from the temple

(11:27-32). Jesus is closer to God and more loved by him than all other men. Consequently he is seated at God's right hand, but not on the throne of God himself.

In the gospel according to *Matthew* the term occurs much more frequently than in Mark. But certainly not with such a sharp profile. In contrast to Mark the term is also applied in the plural to other men (5:9, 45). Although some pronouncements have been added stressing the unique character of the relation between Jesus and the Father (11:27), we can observe at the same time how Matthew remains within the pre-existing Old Testament patterns of thought and applies them to Jesus. Thus from Matt. 16:16, where Peter confesses Jesus as the 'Messiah, Son of the living God', one could conclude that in Matthew both terms are synonymous or equivalent. The author has no problem either with the idea that Jesus was born as king of the Jews (2:2) and emphasises that the entry in Jerusalem must be interpreted as a royal triumphal procession (21:5). A messianic meaning must be thought of also in the case of the temptation narrative.

Apart from the messianic features of the Son of God Matthew also contains other Old Testament meanings. Thus in 2:15 he applies the words of Hosea 11:1 to Jesus. By doing so the book stresses the fact that in Jesus the vicissitudes of Israel, God's beloved Son, are repeated, which also plays a part in the narrative of the temptations which Matthew took over. We already referred to the fact that in the narrative of Jesus' execution the theme of Wisdom 2 is brought out more sharply than in Mark. In as far as we can observe a shift of meaning in comparison with Mark, this takes place in the direction of a closer agreement with the manner in which in the Old Testament the term 'Son of God' is used. A shift in the direction of the pronouncements of Chalcedon I cannot see anywhere. When Peter after his confession in 16:16 is told that it is not flesh and blood, but the father in heaven who has revealed this to him (16:17), this does not necessarily have to have any consequences for the meaning of what Peter said. Neither does the baptismal formula of 28:19, sometimes called trinitarian, witness to such a shift. It does not intend to say anything about Jesus. And even if this were the case, baptism in the name of the Father, the Son and the Holy Spirit does not imply in any way that these three should be equal.[9]

Some of the facts which we mentioned above in respect of Matthew are also to be found in the gospel according to *Luke*. The incorporation of the nativity narratives point to the fact that for Luke, too, the messianic meaning had certainly not lost its validity. If 1:35 must indeed be attributed to Luke himself, it would mean that he himself gave an additional meaning to the term 'Son of God' by relating it to Jesus' birth and descent. But here, too, we should try not to exaggerate. This is clear from the genealogy which Luke includes in 3:23-38. It begins with the words: '. . . Jesus . . . being the son (as was supposed) of Joseph, the son of Heli, the son of Matthat . . .' and ends with: '. . . the son of Enos, the son of Seth, the son of Adam, the son of God.' Though Luke in 1:34 ff. denies the fatherhood to Joseph, the book on the other hand shows Jesus to descend along Joseph's line from David (3:31), the patriarchs (3:34) and through Adam from God, calling them all in passing sons of God.

In the Acts the term only occurs twice. In 9:20 as a recapitulation of Paul's preaching about Jesus. Also in 13:33 in a discourse of Paul who quotes Ps. 2:7 and says that this word from the Scriptures was fulfilled at Jesus' resurrection. Paul's preaching is summarised by Luke in accordance with the old formula included by Paul in Rom. 1:4, where 'sons of God' had a messianic meaning.

3. PAUL'S LETTERS

It is certain that this presentation by Luke does not do justice to Paul, since Rom. 1:3-4 does not express what the title 'Son of God' meant to Paul himself. For it is clear that according to Paul Jesus did not become God's son only at his resurrection, and that he considered Jesus to be God's son in a wider sense than that limited to a messianic function.

First of all we should pay attention to the fact that in the context of Jesus' sonship those who believe in him are also called sons and daughters of God in a sense that surpasses the way in which the Old Testament speaks of men as son or sons of God. Thus Jesus is for Paul the first-born of many brethren (Rom. 8:14, 19; Gal. 3:26). Yet there is a difference between the first-born and those born after him. The latter, for example, are called 'children (*tekna*) of God' (Rom. 8:16-17, 21; 9:8; the former is never given that name). And again he uses the term 'adoption' (*huiothesia*, Rom. 8:15, 23; Eph. 1:5) only for the latter. They have been received by the Spirit at baptism and adopted as children of God. It is this spirit of Jesus that changes men and makes them into children of God, who just like Jesus invoke God as 'Abba'. Just like Jesus, but evidently not on the same grounds and with the same right. Whereas Christians are God's adopted children, Jesus is so in a different way. In which sense, then, is he God's son? Three component meanings are of great importance here. The first two are also to be found in the New Testament passages we already discussed, the third one is new.

The first meaning is that of the sending of God's son: when the fullness of time had come God sent his only son to redeem us (Rom. 8:3; Gal. 4:4-6). It has been argued that Paul here uses a pre-existing pattern of thought and possibly even an existing formula in which the pre-existence of God's son would be presupposed.[10] In that case, however, we would have to reckon seriously with the possibility that Paul himself, too, is thinking of a pre-existing Son of God. But the arguments supporting this opinion do not seem to me to be sufficiently strong. It is more likely that the sending of the son must be seen against the background of the prophets whom God sent before that. The idea is then that God is no longer satisfied with a prophet, but that he sends his own son who is greater than the prophets. Does he send him from heaven? This is not mentioned even once, in contrast to what Wisd. 9:10 says about wisdom. There is no mention either of this son having previously been with God—as is the case with wisdom in Wisd. 9:9. On the contrary, the son who is sent was born under the law, i.e., at a moment when the Torah was already in force, and he was born from a woman (Gal. 4:4); and he is sent when the fullness of time comes. What Paul writes about the sending of the son can in no way be understood of a situation preceding the beginning of history, but rather of an event following Jesus' birth and preceding his resurrection. Sent by God, Jesus, as God's own son, revealed more of God and realised more of God's intentions than any prophet before him, and more, too, than all his predecessors together.

The emphasis with which Paul speaks of God's *own* son is found once more in the second meaning which has to do with the violent end of Jesus' career. Those who killed the prophets also killed Jesus (1 Thess. 2:15). The son was not spared liquidation. With a clear allusion to Gen. 22:12,16, where we are told how God, when Abraham has shown himself prepared to sacrifice his son Isaac, eventually saves the boy, Paul writes that God did not spare his own son, but delivered him up for us all (Rom. 8:32). This must in no way be understood from the viewpoint of later theories of satisfaction. That God sacrificed Jesus is for Paul a proof of the unprecedented great love that God manifests for us all (Rom. 5:8; 8:31; 14:15; 1 Cor. 8:11), a theme we also find in John (John 3:16; 1 John 4:10).

There is a third important meaning, which is characteristic of Pauline theology. Paul brings together the theme of Jesus as son of God and another important theological motif which finds its clearest expression in the words 'image of God'. This motif plays a role in Paul's letters in divergent passages. For our purpose it is important that in different places he calls Jesus the image of God precisely in as far as he is the Son of God (Rom. 8:29; 2 Cor. 4:4, 6; Col. 1:15; see Heb. 1:3) whereas in other places he presupposes this idea (2 Cor. 3:18). God's son is for Paul the visible image of the invisible God. Perhaps one could say that precisely this makes clear to us in which aspect Jesus surpasses the prophets. For he has in common with them that he announces a message and that because of his unwelcome message he is silenced and executed. But to this preponderantly auditive reality this third meaning adds a visual element (2 Cor. 4:4-6; Col. 1:15; 2 Cor. 3:18): the invisible God becomes recognisable in what Jesus does and in what happens to him. As the image, metaphor, likeness and mirror, the son shows who and how God is and what he is prepared to do for us in his love. As often happens, the son's face shows the father's features.

This third meaning takes the theology of Paul further than that of the Synoptic Gospels. But of pre-existence and equality of being with God we cannot discover any trace in Paul's letters. On the contrary, for equality of being is incompatible with the thought that the Son of God is the image of his father. There is only one problem, namely that if we accept a certain punctuation of Rom. 9:5, Jesus would have been called God (*theos*) by Paul. Does this mean that the choice of another punctuation—both grammatically and syntactically perfectly possible—would be nothing else but an easy way out of a difficulty? I do not think so, for we have to remember that the old upper case manuscripts were not punctuated at all.

Summarising we can say that the Son of God makes more of God audible and visible than anybody or anything else, and that consequently he is the first-born of the whole of creation (Col. 1:15). Thus he is more than all other creatures. But he remains less than God. When Paul in 1 Cor. 15:27 applies the words 'all things are put in subjection under him' (Ps. 8:7) to the Son of God, he makes an express exception for God himself and ends with: 'When all things are subjected to him, then the Son himself will also be subjected to him who put all things under him, that God may be everything to everyone.'

4. THE JOHANNINE GOSPEL AND FIRST LETTER

In the writings of John the title 'the Son (of God)' occurs very frequently and occupies a very conspicuous place. This is clear, for example, from the original ending of the gospel (John 20:31) and the final sentences of 1 John (5:19-20). The confession of Jesus is pre-eminently couched in terms of his being the Son of God (1:34, 49; 11:27; 20:31; 1 John 4:15; 5:5, 10, 13). That this belief separates those who are saved from those who are damned is made explicit both in the gospel and in the letter: 'He who believes in the Son has eternal life; he who does not obey the Son shall not see life' (3:36; see 3:18; 6:40). 'No one who denies the Son has the Father. He who confesses the Son has the Father also' (1 John 2:23; 3:23; 4:11-15; 5:5, 11-12). Sometimes this description of Jesus is accompanied by 'King of Israel' (1:49) or 'the Messiah' (11:27), but this happens only when the speakers are Jewish believers.

John has this in common with Paul, that he mentions repeatedly that God sent his son in order that we might believe in him and through this belief have life (John 3:17, 34; 5:36-38; 6:29, 57; 7:28-29; 8:42; 10:34-36; 11:28, 42; 17:3, 8, 18, 21, 23, 25; 20:21; John 4:9-10). In one of these places John does not speak of sending but of giving (John 3:16) and the context (especially verses 14-15) makes it clear that here John is speaking of Jesus' death. For the rest this aspect is hardly mentioned in connection with Jesus as Son of God (see also 1 John 4:9-10).

Of much greater importance are those places in the writings of John which are mentioned as the starting-point and destination of Jesus' mission. As destination John invariably mentions the 'world' (*kosmos*) (3:17; 10:36; 17:18; with 'to come' 1:9; 3:19; 6:14; 9:39; 11:27; 12:46; 18:28). Now it is quite possible to be sent into the world while oneself hailing from this world. But Jesus is repeatedly said not to be of this world (John 8:23; 17:14, 160). He comes from heaven (3:13-16, 31-36; 6:30-51 and of this passage especially verses 38-40), i.e., from God (6:46; 8:38, 42, 47; 14:10-11; 16:27-28; 17:5). What does this 'from God' mean? Did Jesus indeed call God his father in such a way that he made himself equal with God (5:18)? Was it somewhat blasphemous that Jesus called himself God's son (10:36)?

At any rate the Jesus of the fourth gospel says that by virtue of his origin he is closer to God than anyone else and that he remains united to God. He is above all men as the one who comes from above, from heaven (3:31). Up on high with God he has heard and seen (1:18; 3:11, 32; 6:46). In this way he knows the one who sent him (7:28-29; 8:14, 55; 17:25). Consequently, as the one sent by the father he does not speak on his own account, but he says what he has seen and heard (3:11; 7:16; 8:26, 28, 38; 14:24), speaks words of God (3:34) and performs the tasks which the father entrusts to him (5:36; 9:4; 10:32, 37).

But this close bond between the father and the son is not only caused by the son's origin. The hearing and seeing of what the father says and does still continues (5:19; 8:55). Father and son are one (10:30; 17:11, 21-23). The father is in such a way in Jesus and the Son in God that they are inseparable and that their acts and their words cannot be distinguished (14:10, 11, 20; 17:21-23). Who knows and sees the son, knows and sees the father, and who does not know him, does not know the father either (8:19; 14:7-9).

Jesus was from the beginning with God through the word that became flesh in him (1:1, 14). Other mysterious utterances speak of Jesus' own pre-existence (1:15; 8:58; 12:41), which reaches back to before Abraham (8:58).

We are now only one step removed from the pronouncement that the son who comes from the father was also born of the father from the beginning. This step is a very obvious one to take when we elaborate the metaphorical utterances about father and son. Has this been inserted into John? I do not think so. Strangely enough even of the *logos* John does not say that he was born of God. What about the son? The expression 'being born of God' occurs regularly but it is used only of Christians (John 1:13; 1 John 2:29; 3:9; 4:7; 5:1, 4, 18), never of the son Jesus—neither is this the case in 1 John 5:18.[11] Thus only Christians are called children (*tekna*) of God and never sons (John 1:12; 11:52; 1 John 3:1, 2, 10; 5:2), and Jesus is never called a child but Son of God. True enough he is sometimes called the only begotten (*monogenês* 1:14, 18; 3:16, 18), but here the accent is rather on the first than on the second half of the word, which says that he is God's *only* son. Which leaves us to deal finally with the way in which certain versions have translated John 1:18. They translate: 'No one has ever seen God; the only Son, who is in the bosom of the Father, he has made him known.' But this translation is evidently wrong and expresses something that is not there. The son is here said to be reclining in the bosom of the father, like the beloved disciple in Jesus' bosom (13:23); he is said to be the bosom-friend, who is close to the father's heart. As a result our conclusion must be that the writings of John do not mention even once the son's origin or birth from the father. And if we remember that on the contrary this is indeed being said of Christians, we may conclude that in respect of Jesus or the son John avoids this manner of speaking. Did he perhaps want to avoid crossing a certain boundary?

There is at all events another boundary which he did cross. Jesus is unambiguously called God (1:18; 20:21; 1 John 5:20). Only, is this really as unambiguous as it looks? For if on the one hand the use of the predicate 'God' for Jesus implies equality between father and son, there are other places where inequality is expressed just as clearly (e.g., 5:26; 17:3). When Jesus after his resurrection says: 'I am ascending to my Father and your Father, to my God and your God' (20:17), John surely situates even the risen Son of God squarely on the side of us, human beings, over against the father? And 14:28 says plainly: 'The father is greater than I.' Does this then deny the validity of the predicate

'God' for Jesus, the Son of God? It does not. But the ambiguity caused by this reminds us ineluctably that someone calling Jesus God speaks in metaphors just as much, and perhaps even more so, than one who calls him lamb, the way, the truth, the light, the vine and the bread.

5. CONCLUSION

To end with we cast a short glance both before and after the New Testament. What is it that strikes us most when we view the New Testament use of 'Son of God' against the background of the Old Testament? In my opinion it is the fact that this title is filled with the story of someone's life. It is precisely the story that is expressed in the parable of the vineyard. In this parable the link is completed between the pre-existing meanings and the new meaning which is now added: sent by God, the last messenger, of a different order and nature than the ones preceding him, resembling God more closely than anyone else and more united to him than all others, nonetheless or precisely for that reason not spared but killed, then avenged and confirmed by God, become the corner-stone in the new order initiated by God. We do not know who told this story for the first time. Possibly Jesus himself. But even if this is not so it does not matter very much. For he lived the story and died in the process.

If we look ahead we should do so right up to the present day. But since we have to limit ourselves we will not look further ahead than as far as Chalcedon. As one engrossed in the New Testament I once more read attentively the definition of faith of Chalcedon, aware all the time of my lack of competence to comment on it as an expert. My honest reaction was and still is one of dread and consternation. The language used is miles away from anything that has to do with living experience. The abstract words (godhead, humanity, rational soul, consubstantial, inseparable, person, hypostasis) make clear that this was an attempt to reach a kind of philosophical exactitude and clarity of concepts. I suppose that it may have produced certain gains. But I am afraid that it has also inflicted heavy losses. This language makes it virtually impossible to understand the expression 'Jesus is the Son of God' any longer as a metaphor, which is my opinion it undeniably is. And even if the fathers of Chalcedon really did not want to say anything else but that Jesus was simultaneously truly man and truly God, we are still facing serious problems. For such a pronouncement suggests that both predicates have the same linguistic status, and it makes us forget that the predicate 'God' can only be used tautologically or metaphorically.

Notes

1. See further in E. Schweizer, article on *huios ktl, Theol. Wörterbuch z.N.T.* VIII 367-380.

2. See H. Schürmann 'Das Lukasevangelium '*Herders Theol. Komm. z.N.T.* III/1 (Freiburg etc. 1969) p. 55 note 109 with references.

3. Thus U. Wilckens 'Der Brief an die Römer' *Ev. Kath. Komm. z.N.T.* VI/1 (Zürich etc. 1978) pp. 59-60.

4. B. van Iersel '*Der Sohn*' *in den synoptischen Jesusworten* (Leiden [2]1964).

5. That this was a divergent manner of speaking is denied by G. Vermes *Jesus the Jew* (London 1973) pp. 210-211. The text quoted in defence of his view was already known and does not justify this conclusion.

6. These two titles do not have a diverging pre-history. See B. van Iersel *loc. cit.* p. 191.

7. In Mark 1:1 *Christos* in my opinion no longer means 'Messiah', but it has become a part of Jesus' name.

8. See about this especially K. H. Rengstorf, in his article 'apostolos' *Theol. Wörterbuch z.N.T.* I pp. 414-420.

9. A different view is held by Th. de Kruijf *Der Sohn des Lebendigen Gottes* (Rome 1962) pp. 112-115.

10. Thus E. Schweizer, *loc. cit.* pp. 376-378.

11. For the arguments see R. Schnackenburg 'Die Johannesbriefe' *Herders Theol. Komm. z.N.T.* XIII/3 (Freiburg 1953) pp. 251-252. However, about John 1:13: see P. Hofrichter *Nich aus Blut sondern monogen aus Gott geboren* (Würzburg 1978) who holds egennêthê for the correct reading.

Literature

The most important recent literature is quoted in the notes to McDermott, J. M. *Jesus and the Son of God Title* Gregorianum 62 (1981) pp. 277-318.

To this the following recent publications could be added: de Jonge, M. *Stranger from Heaven and Son of God* (Missoula 1977). *The myth of God Incarnate* ed. John Hick (London 1977), especially the articles contributed by F. Young and M. Goulder. Vellanickal, M. *The Divine Sonship of Christians in the Johannine writings* (Rome 1977).

Byrne, B. *Sons of God—Seed of Abraham* (Rome 1979).

Kazmierski, C. R. *Jesus the Son of God* (Würzburg 1979).

de Ru, G. 'Jezus de Zoon van God' *Theologia Reformata* XXIII (1980) 78-92.

Geoffrey Wainwright

'Son of God' in Liturgical Doxologies

1. SYSTEMATIC QUESTIONS

ORTHODOX CHRISTIANS as well as Arians and other Christological reductionists all agree that Christ is mediator between God and man in salvation and worship: he mediates God's blessings to humans, and he mediates human thanksgiving to God. The decisive question is whether, or in what sense(s), Christ is *also*, and perhaps *first*, a proper recipient of doxology. Does the undoubted humanity of Christ provide an exhaustive account of his person, so that to doxologise him is formally to fall into creature-worship or idolatry? Or was, and is, his mediation such that it led God, and leads Christians, to confer on Christ a divine status which required, and expresses, our worship of him? Or is Christ's mediation between God and man such as could only derive, ontologically, from his being divine, so that he receives worship by eternal right? In terms of 'the Son of God' in liturgical doxology: is the title *merely* 'functional', so that any ascription of praise to 'the Son' is not made at all strictly but somehow accrues to Christ the man from his mediatorial role in salvation and prayer? Or is the title an adoptive one which corresponds to the divine dignity to which Christ has been elevated? Or is 'the Son' the second person of the blessed Trinity, who for us men and for our salvation became incarnate and now receives the worship of believers?

Let us listen to the liturgical witness of the Church, noting the theological understanding which has accompanied the cultic formularies. In this way we can gather the data supplied by the principles of *lex orandi*, *lex credendi* towards the answering of the systematic questions concerning the Son of God.

2. THE APOSTOLIC CHURCH

According to Rom. 15:6, God is to be glorified as 'the God and Father of our Lord Jesus Christ'. In Rom. 1:8, Paul thanks God 'through Jesus Christ' (*dia* + genitive). The same construction is used in the doxology of Rom. 16:27, which may not be original, and in the Amen-saying of 2 Cor. 1:19 f., where Christ is called Son of God (see Rom. 1:9). It is exegetically controversial whether Rom. 9:5 is to be so punctuated as to make Paul bless the divine name of Christ, though the *consensus patrum* takes the verse that

49

way.[1] Exegetes also argue about the extent to which the phrase 'designated Son of God in power by his resurrection from the dead' would be understood in an adoptionist sense by the apostle himself as well as in the liturgical text from which he is quoting (Rom. 1:3 f.). The 'sending of God's own Son', in Rom. 8:3, is more congruous with the pre-existence of Christ. Certainly 'his own Son', whom 'God did not spare but gave him up for us all', is now our heavenly Intercessor (Rom. 8:31-34). It is by 'the Spirit of sonship' that we call God 'Abba' (Rom. 8:14-17; Gal. 4:4-7): we are now *filii in Filio* (see Gal. 3:26), and it is in this sense that God's Son has become the first-born of many brethren (Rom. 8:29).

In 1 Tim. 2:1-8, in the course of an admonition to prayer, 'the man Christ Jesus' is called the 'one mediator between God and men' on account of his gift of himself 'as a ransom for all'. The reference to Christ's humanity without his divinity did not prevent Pius XII from borrowing the text to begin his 1947 encyclical on Christian worship, *Mediator Dei*. In the Christological hymn of 1 Tim. 3:16 the pre-existence of Christ is at least adumbrated: one should at least read 'who' (masculine), not 'which' (neuter); and some manuscripts indeed read '*God* was manifested in the flesh . . .'. In 2 Tim. 4:18, 'the Lord' to whom glory is ascribed may be Christ. In Titus 3:4-7, it is 'through (*dia*) Jesus Christ our Saviour' that God has poured out the Holy Spirit upon us.

According to Eph. 1:3-14, God has blessed us with all spiritual blessings 'in Christ'. 'Through Christ' we have access to the Father in the one Spirit (2:18). Glory is ascribed to God 'in the church and in Christ Jesus' (3:21). In a eucharistic passage, Col. 1:12-14 thanks the Father for transferring us 'to the kingdom of his beloved Son, in whom we have redemption'; and in the ensuing Christological hymn, all things were created through Christ and for Christ, 'in whom all the fullness of God was pleased to dwell, and through him to reconcile all things to himself' (1:15-20).

In 1 Pet. 1:3 ff. God is blessed for what he has done for us through Christ. We are to offer spiritual sacrifices to God 'through Christ' (2:5). In the exercise of gifts, God is to be glorified 'through Jesus Christ' (4:11). By 2 Pet. 3:18 the glory is ascribed to 'our Lord and Saviour Jesus Christ'.

In *Hebrews*, Christ appears predominantly as the high priest who, having made the sacrifice of obedience, entered heaven as our forerunner and intercessor. We are now able to 'draw near' to God 'through' Christ (7:25; 10:19-22; 13:15). Jesus, our great high priest, is 'the Son of God' (4:14). He is the same Son by whom God spoke to us in these last days (1:2); through whom also he created the world (*ibid.*); who radiates the glory of God (1:3); and who may, in a quotation from Ps. 45, himself be addressed as 'God' (1:8).[2] In 13:20 f. it is uncertain whether the glory is ascribed to the Father or to Christ.

In the fourth gospel, Jesus teaches the disciples to pray 'in his name' (15:16; 16:23 f., see 14:13 f.; 16:26 f.). After his resurrection he is acclaimed by Thomas as 'My Lord and my God' (20:28). In the hymnic prologue, he is called *theos* (1:1), and all things were made through him (1:3). The only Son (some manuscripts read God), who is in the bosom of the Father, has made God known (1:18). He has glorified God on earth, and at the end he prays God to 'glorify me in thy own presence with the glory which I had with them before the world was made' (17:4 f.). In Rev. 1:5 f. and 5:11-14, glory is ascribed to him by the Church as royal priesthood and by every creature.

We may conclude that the Church of the New Testament knew Christ not only as the mediator between God and man in salvation and worship but also as himself, in a rich variety of ways, the object of cultic honour. The latter status was recognised to him as soon as the title *Kyrios* was used with the kind of charge attaching to it in the hymn of Phil. 2:5-11; and already in Aramaic the title *Mar* (as in *Maranatha*, 1 Cor. 16:22) could bear divine meaning.[3] We have also seen enough pre-existence language to be sure that the apostolic Church could not remain satisfied—if ever it was satisfied—with an account that made of Christ a man 'adopted' by God.

3. BEFORE ARIUS

A difficulty arises from the fact that patristic and liturgical doxologies were susceptible to change by copyists; but we shall do our best with some representative specimens.[4]

In *Didachè* 9 and 10, the Father is thanked for benefits he has made known to us 'through your Child (*Pais*) Jesus'; and, at least in 9:4, glory is ascribed to God 'through Jesus Christ'. At his martyrdom, bishop Polycarp prayed a *eucharistia*: 'Lord God almighty, Father of your beloved and blessed Child (*Pais*) Jesus Christ, through whom we received knowledge of you. . . . For this and all things I praise you, I bless you, I glorify you through the eternal and heavenly high priest, Jesus Christ, your beloved Child, through whom glory be to you [with him and the Holy Spirit] now and for all the ages to come' (*Martyrdom of Polycarp*, 14). In the so-called *Apostolic Tradition* of Hippolytus, the eucharistic anaphora begins: 'We thank you, God, through your beloved Child (*puer*) Jesus Christ, whom in the last times you sent to us as saviour and redeemer and angel of your will; who is your inseparable Word, through whom you made all things, and in whom you were well pleased; whom you sent from heaven into the Virgin's womb; and who, conceived in the womb, was made flesh and was manifested as your Son. . . .' It concludes: '. . . in order that we may praise and glorify you through your Child (*puer*) Jesus Christ, through whom be glory and honour to you [to the Father and the Son with the Holy Spirit in your holy Church] both now and to the ages of ages.' In each case, there is scholarly controversy over the authenticity of the bracketed trinitarian formula; though some argue that the expressions in the latter case agree with Hippolytus' theology and usage elsewhere. The trinitarian formulation harmonises with the type employed (to the pleasant surprise of St Basil a century later) by Denis of Alexandria, c. 262: 'Having received from the presbyters who preceded us a formula and rule, we conclude our present letter with those words by which we, like them, make our thanksgiving: To God the Father and the Son our Lord Jesus Christ with the Holy Spirit be glory and might for ever and ever.'

That Christ should *receive* as well as mediate worship finds Origen's theoretical disapproval. In strict speech (*kyrolexia*), says Origen in his treatise *On Prayer* and in the *Contra Celsum*, prayer is offered only to the Father 'through' Christ. If prayer is improperly or in a secondary sense (*katachrêstikôs*) offered to Christ, it is so that the Son and high priest may convey it to the Father. This corresponds to Origen's rigorously subordinationist view whereby Christ is *theos*, but not *ho theos*. Yet Origen concluded his own sermons with doxologies addressed to Christ. Here the preacher was coming closer to the devotional life of the Church.[5] The martyrs, following Stephen (Acts 7:59), prayed to Christ.[6] Hymns start to be addressed to Christ, such as the one with which Clement closes his *Paidagogos* and also the famous 'Phôs hilaron':

O gracious Light,
pure brightness of the everliving Father in heaven,
O Jesus Christ, holy and blessed!
Now as we come to the setting of the sun,
and our eyes behold the vesper light,
we sing your praises, O God: Father, Son and Holy Spirit.
You are worth at all times to be praised by happy voices,
O Son of God, O Giver of life,
and to be glorified through all worlds.

4. AFTER ARIUS

T. E. Pollard has shown the tension in Origen between his middle-platonist solution to the *metaphysical* problem of relating God and the created cosmos, of relating the One and the Many—which led him to take Logos as the regulative concept for Christ—and, on the other hand, his *religious* and *theological* concept of the Son. The task was bequeathed to the generation of Athanasius, stimulated by the Arian error, to make *the Son*—now not so much a cosmological as rather a soteriological postulate—the regulative concept. In this, says Pollard, 'Athanasius is ultimately the defender, not of Origenism of the right wing, but of the "simple faith" of the Church—embodied in the *regula fidei* and catechetical instruction—in Jesus Christ as the Eternal Son of God who has accomplished for men what only God can do in saving them from their sin, recreating in them the defaced or destroyed image of God, and reconciling them to God the Father. Only one who is eternally God and yet at the same time really Incarnate as man can save mankind.'[7]

In his soteriological arguments against Arian views of both Son and Spirit, Athanasius appealed to the threefold name confessed and pronounced in baptism, the sacrament of salvation.[8] He argued further from the liturgical life of the Church, when he maintained that the Church's worship of Christ would constitute idolatry if the Son were not God.[9] But Arians did, in fact, appeal to Catholic liturgy in support of their own position. Thus an Arian from North Italy or the Danube[10] argued that 'the Catholics themselves in their oblations put the Father before the Son by saying "It is right and fitting that we should give thanks to you here and everywhere, holy Lord, almighty God; and there is no one through whom we can have access to you, pray to you, offer a sacrifice to you, except the one whom you sent to us. . .".' The classic answer from the orthodox side was given by St Basil in his treatise *On the Holy Spirit*.

Basil does not disavow the doxology addressed to the Father through (*dia*) the Son in (*en*) the Holy Spirit. Just as God's blessings descend to us through the Son in the Spirit, so it is appropriate that our thanksgiving in the Spirit mounts to the Father through the Son. But to the indivisibility of God's operations towards the world there corresponds, in the teaching of the Cappadocians, the mutual indwelling of the three divine hypostases. When, therefore, God is contemplated in himself, it is proper to give glory to the Father with (*meta*) the Son with (*syn*) the Holy Spirit. It is his own use of this form which Basil defends against the Macedonians.[11]

Some of Basil's claimed liturgical precedents antedate the Arian controversy. Particularly interesting is his report that the Christians of Mesopotamia were obliged on linguistic grounds to 'offer the doxology by the syllable "and"'. The Syrian evidence goes back to the *Didascalia Apostolorum* in the third century: 'We have fixed and determined that you shall worship God [the Father] almighty and Jesus, [his Son] the Christ, and the Holy Spirit.'[12] A completely co-ordinated form became common in the Byzantine liturgy, e.g.: 'For you are a good and benevolent God, and to you we send up the glory, to the Father and to the Son and to the Holy Spirit, now and always and in all eternity.'

The defeat of Arianism will have facilitated the introduction of hymns glorifying Christ into the principal liturgy of the Church. To the late fourth century belong, for instance, the *Gloria in Excelsis* (the arianising author of *Apostolic Constitutions* turns the whole address towards the Father of Christ, but it is likely that the Christologically-addressed central part was the original core of the hymn)[13] and the *Te Deum*, with its middle section:

You, Christ, are the king of glory,
the eternal Son of the Father.
When you became man to set us free,
you did not shun the Virgin's womb.

The Byzantines introduced the *Monogenês* hymn, attributed to the emperor Justinian, at the opening of the liturgy:

> Only-begotten Son and Word of God, who being immortal yet didst deign for our salvation to be incarnate of the holy Mother of God and Ever-Virgin Mary, and without change didst become man and wast crucified, Christ our God, and by death didst overcome death, being One of the Holy Trinity and glorified together with the Father and the Holy Spirit: Save us.

In the monophysite churches, parts even of the anaphora came to be addressed to the Son; although Cyril of Alexandria, whom the monophysites claimed as one of their own, ascribed to the human mind of Christ, as T. F. Torrance has shown, an important role as that which allows Christ to take up the Church's worship into his own worship of the Father.[14]

In the West, the Roman Mass continued to be offered 'through Christ our Lord'; and Christ was still seen as mediator of God's blessings to humanity, as in the *per quem haec omnia, Domine, semper bona creas, sanctificas, vivificas, benedicis, et praestas nobis* at the end of the canon. The doxology after the psalms was spoken in the form *Gloria Patri et Filio et Spiritui Sancto*, to which the Council of Vaison in 529 added the *sicut erat in principio et nunc et semper et in saecula saeculorum*, in order to refute the Arians who 'blasphemously' held that the Son 'had a beginning' rather than 'having been with the Father always'. It was for similar reasons that the *per Jesus Christum [Filium tuum] Dominum nostrum* at the end of prayers received the addition of *qui tecum vivit et regnat in unitate Spiritus Sancti*. Arianism lingered with the Goths in Spain and Gaul; and it is in face of this threat, and of a recurrent adoptionism, that Mozarabic and Gallican liturgies contain many presidential prayers addressed to the Son, even in parts of the eucharistic prayer.[15] The 'Athanasian Creed' is a western composition: 'Now this is the Catholic faith, that we worship one God in Trinity and Trinity in unity. . . .'

The Protestant Reformation did little to alter the picture whereby Christ was both mediator and object of worship; though the Anglican *Book of Common Prayer* did, for instance, re-direct a few prayers to the Father instead of the Son.[16] Thanks to the magisterial work of J. A. Jungmann on *The Place of Christ in Liturgical Prayer*,[17] the modern liturgical movement has re-emphasized the address of prayer to God through Christ. Jungmann's laudable concern was to recover the soteriological and liturgical importance of Christ's humanity (instead of letting it be marginalised in para-liturgical devotions); and it would be wrong to suspect him, or the authorised revisers of the official liturgies, of Christological reductionism. But as long as Arians and Adoptionists remain alive and well, it would be unwise to fetter the Church's instinct to address praise and prayer to Christ as well as to the Father.

5. SYSTEMATIC CONCLUSIONS

In light of the liturgical witness, 'the Son' is best regarded as the ultimate self-gift of God to the world. In the words of the oldest form of the anaphora of St Basil: 'In these last days you manifested to us who sat in darkness and the shadow of death your only-begotten Son, our Lord and God and Saviour, Jesus Christ. . . . He loved his own who were in the world, and for our salvation gave himself to death. . . .' Or in the Byzantine anaphora of St John Chrysostom: 'Holy are you and all-holy, and magnificent is your glory, for you so loved the world that you gave your only-begotten Son that all who believe in him should not perish but have eternal life.' As the ultimate self-gift of God to the world, the Son is readily considered as the mediator also of all God's other benefits to us. Since it is only as *filii in Filio*, redeemed and transformed, that we may give God due worship, it is inevitable that Christ be also the mediator of our praise and prayers. And it is because the Son is, both towards the world and within the Trinity, *God-as-self-given*, that the Church has doxologised him. The self-giving Father remains, in Cappadocian terms, 'the fount of divinity'.[18]

Notes

1. For an exegesis in this sense, see B. M. Metzger 'The punctuation of Rom. 9:5' in *Christ and Spirit in the New Testament* eds. B. Lindars and S. Smalley (Cambridge 1973) pp. 95-112.

2. For this exegesis, see R. E. Brown *Jesus God and Man* (Milwaukee 1967).

3. M. Black in Lindars and Smalley, cited in note 1, pp. 189-196.

4. See J. Lebreton *Histoire du dogme de la Trinité* (Paris 1928) II pp. 618-630 (and already pp. 174-247); F. Cabrol 'La Doxologie dans la prière chrétienne des premiers siècles' *Recherches de Science Religieuse* 18 (1928) 9-30; J. M. Hanssens *La Liturgie d'Hippolyte* (Rome 1959) pp. 343-370, and *La Liturgie d'Hippolyte* (Rome 1970) pp. 167-259; A. Stuiber 'Doxologie' in *Realenzyklopädie für Antike und Christentum* IV (Stuttgart 1959) columns 210-226.

5. See J. Lebreton 'Le Désaccord de la foi populaire et de la théologie savante dans l'Église chrétienne du IIIe siècle' *Revue d'Histoire Ecclésiastique* 19 (1923) 481-506, and 20 (1924) 5-37.

6. K. Baus 'Das Gebet der Märtyrer' in *Trierer Theologische Zeitschrift* 62 (1953) 19-32.

7. T. E. Pollard 'Logos and Son in Origen, Arius and Athanasius' in *Studia Patristica* II (Berlin 1957) pp. 282-287. A. Heron suggests that the passage through the Logos-theology of the Apologists helped to 'demythologise' the notion of Son: 'Logos, Image, Son: some models and paradigms in early Christology' *Creation, Christ and Culture* ed. R. W. A. McKinney (Edinburgh 1976) pp. 43-62.

8. For example, Anthanasius *Letters to Serapion* I, 24 and 29 f. (PG 26, 597-600); see Basil *On the Holy Spirit* paragraphs 24-26, 28, 34-36.

9. For example, Athanasius *Ad Adelphium* 3 (PG 26, 1,074-1,077).

10. G. Mercati *Antiche reliquie liturgiche* (Rome 1902) pp. 45-71.

11. For the distinction between the two forms and the justification of both, see especially paragraphs 16, 63 and 68.

12. *Didascalia Apostolorum* ed. R. H. Connolly (Oxford 1929) p. 204 f.

13. B. Cappelle 'Le Texte du *Gloria in excelsis*' *Revue d'Histoire Ecclésiastique* 44 (1949) 439-457.

14. T. F. Torrance *Theology in Reconciliation* (London 1975) pp. 139-214: 'The mind of Christ in worship: the problem of apollinarianism in the liturgy.'

15. J. A. Jungmann *Liturgisches Erbe und Pastorale Gegenwart* (Innsbruck 1960) pp. 3-86: 'Die Abwehr des germanischen Arianismus . . .'. Pollard, *loc. cit.*, rightly states that all Arius does is to 'transfer the adoptianism of Paul of Samosata to the pre-mundane sphere'.

16. J. Dowden *The Workmanship of the Prayer Book* (London [2]1904) pp. 127-129, and *Further Studies in the Prayer Book* (London 1908) pp. 286-295.

17. *Die Stellung Christi im liturgischen Gebet* (Münster 1925; [2]1962).

18. The systematic position is more fully developed in my book *Doxology* (London and New York 1980) chapter 2.

Tarsicius van Bavel

Chalcedon: Then and Now

HISTORY SHOWS that every general Council always ends up with a compromise. The final document of each Council always reveals an attempt to maintain unity by making concessions to conflicting trends current in the Church at the time. This is why one should never try to interpret conciliar statements by glossing over the inherent difficulties or by wild generalisations. On the contrary, the original tensions, contained in the framing of the text, should be respected because they simply reflect man's difficulty in coping with faith as he experiences it—his reason struggles, like Jacob, with the angel of faith. No human reason can fully articulate or assimilate the mystery of the faith. This is the reason why the discovery of such tensions is not harmful but rather salutary for the act of faith.

1. THE TENSION IN THE FORMULATION OF THE CREED OF CHALCEDON (451)

We know that the bishops who took part in the Council of Chalcedon fiercely opposed the demands of the Emperor's delegation to draft a new creed. They thought that the creeds of Nicea (325) and the first Council of Constantinople (381) were quite satisfactory. If in the end, they yielded to pressure, they did so doubtless with the intention to make sure that the faith remained one 'because since (the last Council) there had been people whose teaching on Jesus Christ affected the whole matter of salvation' (see Denzinger-Schönmetzer, *Enchiridion Symbolorum* Herder1964, sections 301 and 302, which has the Greek text and a Latin translation).

Here we give a translation of the actual text as literally as we could manage (subdivided and numbered for easy reference): '(1) Following the holy Fathers, (2) confessing as one and the same Son, (3) our Lord Jesus Christ, (4) is what we all teach, (5) he is fully divine and (6) fully human, (7) truly God and truly man, (8) with a rational soul and a body; (9) as divine he is one with the Father and (10) as one who is human he is one with us, (11) "like us in all things except for sin"; (12) as divine he was born of the Father before the ages, (13) but in the last days, (14) he is the same who for us and for our salvation was born (15) of the virgin Mary, mother of God in his humanity; (16) the one and the same Christ, Son, Lord, Only-begotten, (17) is to be acknowledged to be in two natures (18) without mixture or change, without division or separation; (19) the distinction between the two natures is never taken away by their being united, (20) on the contrary, the specific quality of both natures is maintained, (21) even in the concurrence in one person and one hypostasis, (22) and he is not shared between or divided into two persons (23) but is one and the same Son, (24) God, Word, Lord Jesus Christ; (25) thus we were taught about him by the prophets of old and (26) by Jesus Christ himself, (27) and this is what has been transmitted to us in the symbol of the Fathers.'

To understand this definition one has to see it in its historical perspective. The earliest causes which led in the end to Chalcedon were varied: docetism and gnosticism reduced Jesus' humanity to a mere appearance of humanity; the Arians denied his being equal with the Father, and the Apollinarians maintained that the Logos took the place of the human spirit in Jesus. The more immediate history of Chalcedon, however, began with the Council of Ephesus in 431. There the whole emphasis was put on the oneness of the Son of God against Nestorius who refused to put his being begotten of the Father on the same line as his being born of Mary. Nor did he want to put Jesus' being 'one with the Father' on the same basis as his being 'one with us'. Because of this he maintained that one could not attribute Jesus' birth of Mary to the divine Word. Over against this Ephesus maintained that Jesus Christ cannot be divided into two subjects.

This emphasis on the unity of Christ by the Council of Ephesus brought the problem which faced the Council of Chalcedon right into the open: how could a human being who is the only-begotten Son of God still be a real human being? How could Jesus' experience as a true human being avoid being wholly absorbed by his divinity? This problem became even more sharply pointed by the teaching of Eutyches and Dioscorus of Alexandria, which became the immediate occasion for the Council of Chalcedon. There is, of course, the question whether Eutyches was properly understood by his contemporaries. The fact is that they reproached him for not doing full justice to the full humanity of Jesus. According to him Christ was not the same as us as we really are. He indeed had a human body but this was not due to his sharing our species in substance. Both Eutyches and Dioscorus were taken to be confined to the Alexandrian view which was that 'before the incarnation there were two natures, but afterwards there was only one'.

In proceedings in 448 Eutyches was legally condemned. There it was stated as a definition that Christians must confess two natures in Christ also after the incarnation. But already within one year after this, pressure exercised by his powerful patrons had him rehabilitated and the school of Antioch was not only ruled out completely but also accused of Nestorianism.

But with great courage Leo the Great, Bishop of Rome, opposed both Dioscorus and the emperor, and to his great credit, he turned the tide. Influenced by the much more clearly defined terms with which western Christology operated, particularly under the influence of St Augustine, he was also able to provide a clear formulation of the distinction of the natures and the unity of person in Christ. When the Fathers of Chalcedon were confronted with the demand for a new formula, they at first refused, but were then presented with the dilemma: who is right, Leo or Dioscorus? This tipped the balance in Leo's favour, as Dioscorus had already been condemned. In so far as the substance of the issue was concerned all this meant that for the Fathers of Chalcedon the actual situation was as follows. Although for their main inspiration they looked to Alexandria and its Christology, particularly as upheld by Cyril of Alexandria, there was nevertheless a cross-current of Antiochean and western concepts, even though it did not flow very strongly. There is no doubt that Chalcedon was vitally concerned with the fact that Jesus was fully human.

It is true that the definition of Chalcedon starts with the confession of the Lord Jesus Christ as one and the same. This three times repeated 'one and the same' (see nn. 2, 16, 23) covers the whole body of the definition.

But, as one can see in nn. 9 and 10, an almost equal emphasis has been put on the distinction between the two natures. The most original feature of the definition is that it contains so few 'corrections' of the prevalent terminology of Alexandria. And what are those corrections? The first is that 'of two natures' has been changed into 'in two natures' (n. 18). The expression 'of two natures', which almost certainly occurred in a previous draft, was rejected. The rejected formula rightly replaced because it could too easily be explained in a monophysitic sense to the detriment of Jesus' human nature as if in Jesus there was only one nature, namely the divine one. In nn. 19-21 one recognises a quotation from Cyril of Alexandria which is followed by one from Leo the Great: 'On the contrary, the specific quality of both natures is maintained, even in the concurrence in one person and one hypostasis.' Finally, the first draft was reinforced by the addition of four adverbs (here rendered by four adverbial phrases): 'without mixture or change, without division or separation' (*inconfuse, immutabiliter, indivise, inseparabiliter*). Although these qualifications express both the distinction and the unity we see here nevertheless an interesting shift compared with Ephesus. There 'unseparatedly' came first, while in Chalcedon it was 'unmixedly'. Here, then, we have the tension which existed in the formula of Chalcedon.

2. THE MAIN CONCERN OF THE COUNCIL OF CHALCEDON

In Nicea the main burden of the Council had been to ensure that Christ was confessed as the Son of God, one in being with the Father while in Ephesus it was that there is only one Christ. In Chalcedon, however, the main concern was the distinction between the divine and the human nature of Christ. Its specific contribution lay in that it maintained the specific difference between these two although both are joined in one and the same Jesus Christ, not only in his outward manifestation (*prosōpon*) but also in his deeper being (*hypostasis*). In this way Chalcedon managed to bring the two views of Alexandria and Antioch together.

The Alexandrian theologians had been fighting Arianism with might and main because it had concluded from the incarnation that the Son could not be truly God. They had, moreover, been fiercely opposed to Nestorianism because, in their eyes, it sacrificed the unity of Christ in order to prevent a diminution of his humanity. On the other hand, the theologians of Antioch had always strongly opposed any view which threatened to turn Jesus' humanity into a mere sham humanity and were determined to maintain that Jesus really was one of us. So the Council of Chalcedon had to answer the question how we should understand the full unity and the clear distinction between the human and the divine in Christ. The greatest difficulty lay in the terminology although underneath the matter of words there obviously stirred a definite theological concern.

A compromise was found but it meant that the Alexandrians had to abandon their one-nature formula and that in Antioch it was imperative that there was no drifting towards a doctrine of two persons. In this way it became possible to put equal emphasis on the distinction between the human and the divine in Christ and on his personal unity.

Perhaps the best way of looking at the formula of Chalcedon is to contrast it with that of Cyril of Alexandria who spoke of 'the one nature of the Word Incarnate'. His Christology wholly concentrated on the divine Logos; he never put the divine nature 'over against' Christ's human nature. His whole Christology is seen in terms of a 'descent': the divine Word 'descends', 'comes down' to our reality. It hardly needs saying that this leads to the great danger of an exaggerated deification of Jesus' humanity. Actually, the group of Antioch also still thought in terms of a descending God who becomes man. There is no trace of any difference between the two schools in their concept of God. They differed mainly from the Alexandrians in that the theologians of Antioch put the human and the divine nature more, so to speak, 'side by side' in Christ in order to be able to stress more emphatically Christ's equality with us. They saw Jesus' humanity as more independent than the Alexandrians did. This is why Chalcedon brought a re-discovery of the human dimension in Christ. It was a step towards a recognition of the complete humanity of Jesus Christ. And there lies the significance of Chalcedon.

3. THE TENSION WHICH CHALCEDON DID NOT RESOLVE

All Councils have an element of controversy. They are always about definite and widely debated issues and so the answers worked out in a Council are always incomplete and limited. In the same way those that took part in the Council of Chalcedon had no intention of saying everything that could be said about Christ. Nor did they think it their business to give people a lecture in metaphysics. The ideas they used were based on current popular philosophical understanding; they were not meant to be the expression of scientific exactitude. The terms used still had some kind of general meaning. In fact, many bishops who were present felt that the terminology was a kind of ballast and voiced this when they said explicitly that the fourth Council was no basis for baptismal catechesis. They saw the formulation mainly as a stick to belabour heresies with. The new ideas should not become the most important matter. And here we have already a clear warning that future generations should not overrate the terminology used by Chalcedon.

According to A. de Halleux there are at least three points where the Chalcedon formula is doctrinally inaccurate. They are: (a) it does not say Christ is one hypostasis, but only that there is one hypostasis after the two natures have been united; (b) it does not say that this hypostasis must be understood as a person in our modern sense of the word; (c) nor does it say explicitly that this person is the divine Logos.

Yet, the wrong conclusions were certainly drawn from Chalcedon later on. But, obviously such conclusions are already a form of interpreting the Chalcedon formula. At the Council, however, the concept of hypostasis was so ambiguous that any theological school could exploit it for its own purposes. Another weakness lies in the expression 'acknowledged in two natures'. This is wholly in harmony with Cyril's inclination to explain the distinction as based on a logical abstraction. But if the distinction is only seen as depending on an intellectual exercise, then it is bound to undermine the sense of the reality of Jesus' full humanity, as one can see not only in Cyril himself but in the whole of tradition afterwards.

Obviously nobody blames the Fathers of Chalcedon for having used Greek notions that were current at the time. What else could they have done? One may also well maintain that these notions were conditioned by their historical age, and were therefore inadequate, but which notions are not? And so one begins to realise the limitations of the Chalcedon formula.

(a) Chalcedon wanted to find a satisfactory way of expressing what one might call the 'inner constitution' of Jesus Christ: What is the relation between the divine and the human dimensions in him? But in this process a very important section of Christology was practically left out. With the exception of a reference to his birth from the virgin Mary, there is nothing about the historical life of Jesus. There is no mention of his public appearance, suffering, death and resurrection. This produced a view of Jesus Christ which was very different from that of the New Testament where Jesus' identity was mainly revealed through the actual liberation which people experienced in meeting him in his life and behaviour.

It is obviously right that a Council should fix the limits of its main concern, but is it not possible that there are limits which creep in without the participants being aware of them?

In their debates about Jesus Christ the Council Fathers concentrated mainly on the moment of his incarnation. I have a strong hunch that this has something to do with the Greek preference for getting down to the being of things. The unchanging and stable character of 'being' appealed more to the Greeks than the moving, changing, factual and historical features which mark 'becoming'. Therefore the real focus of thinking about Jesus is above all the person of the divine Logos. From there one goes down to the consideration of Jesus as man. But this leads to the tremendous issue whether in that case one can still have a true appreciation of the historical Jesus. In such a view Jesus' humanity is only seen as important in so far as our human reality allows us to see through it and get a glimpse of the divine world, or, more briefly, how far Jesus is only a God made transparent.

But if this is the case, is there any intrinsic value left to Jesus' human existence as such? Does this not imply that the gap between the divine and the human is totally unbridgeable?

The heavy emphasis which Chalcedon put on the incarnation resulted in giving the impression that, according to this model of salvation, everything was already over and done with at the moment that the divine was united with the human. The rest of Jesus' life on earth was pushed into the background. Its formula demands therefore without doubt that it be supplemented by the actual history of salvation. As it stands, the formula remains too abstract and too static.

(*b*) The expression 'in two natures' also puts the distinction in a way which suggests a merely static juxtaposition of the two natures. It leaves out the living and dynamic interrelationship between the human and the divine. Although the Council did not mean this, it might easily lead to the idea of two separate subjects living side by side, even though they exist in a network of communication. The duality slips almost unnoticed into a form of dualism which thinks of the divine and human natures not in terms of being 'in' each other, but in terms of them being 'next to' each other, because in the two natures' pattern both natures retain their own life and activation. The whole tradition, from the Fathers of the Church to today, shows that this has led to such statements as: Jesus knew sorrow according to his human nature but worked miracles according to his divinity. Human weakness and divine glory are divided between his two natures. In practice this inevitably leads to a form of dualism because the implication of such a way of speaking suggests in fact (though not in theory) the notion that each nature leads its own existence.

(*c*) It would also seem that behind the formula of Chalcedon there lies a definite view of God which seems to weigh heavily on the whole subject. And this view influenced the concept of 'divine person' as well as that of 'divine nature'. It bears all the marks of contemporary thought which saw the divine reality as exalted above, and in total contrast to, our human situation. In his being God is eternal, omnipotent, immutable, independent, invulnerable and both unmoved and unmoving. This view of God, which differs sharply from the way we talk today about God as 'vulnerable' or 'compassionate', a God 'in movement', was prevalent in Alexandria as well as in Antioch. The school of Antioch saw in the 'unchanged' situation of both natures a way of keeping the Logos out of all suffering and earthly vicissitudes. It then became an axiom that 'Jesus suffered while remaining invulnerable to suffering'. One cannot help wondering, though, what the 'self-emptying' of Christ (Phil. 2:7) could mean in reality if the divine nature is beyond any change. How seriously did the Council Fathers take the 'being born in the likeness of men' (Phil. 2:7)?

Moreover, this vision led to a rather rash deification of the human dimension in Jesus. The human attributes of Jesus were, so to speak, intercepted and crowded out by the divine attributes. In such a view Jesus is neither dependent nor sad, worried, growing up, changing, ignorant, feeling abandoned or even believing. Even the 'communicatio idiomatum', the assigning of the attributes of both natures to one and the same person, failed to affect this development. We can see this in the fact that the psychology of Jesus as man has remained for centuries the main stumbling-block for any Christology. The question how to reconcile Jesus' complete humanity with all the limitations of a human existence has not been answered.

In spite of its own formula Chalcedon failed to show Jesus as embodying human freedom face to face with the Father. Jesus was not sufficiently shown as a man who in his suffering, anguish, fidelity, faith, obedience and elevation also stood over against God his Father. Jesus' attitude towards his Father cannot be exclusively ascribed to his human nature or be limited to it. It was not a nature which surrendered itself to the Father but Jesus himself. That Jesus himself as man is that Son of God was only poorly brought out in Chalcedon. The 'communicatio idiomatum' is rather an abstract attempt at safeguarding the unity of Christ's person. It remains too much on the level of a concept without too serious consequences for the divine dimension. The human and the divine of Jesus cannot be lifted out of time and put simply side by side. One should rather say that God occurs 'in' the man Jesus. It is the events of Jesus in his actual life which bring out the mysterious unity of the human and the divine in him. It is precisely Jesus' history on this earth which reveals him as the Son of God.

4. THE SIGNIFICANCE OF CHALCEDON TODAY

Chalcedon was a beacon on the way Christology had to go. Its task was to reconcile unity and distinction in Jesus Christ, to affirm an existential identity in a sustained distinction. It pointed the way towards a fuller understanding of the complete humanity of Christ. It sounded a warning for Christians of all times. The human dimension of Jesus must not be allowed to be absorbed by the divine, nor can one sever the man Jesus from his being the Son of God. Any exaggeration in one direction or the other is wrong because it would diminish the incarnation of God. In modern parlance: Christology must not shrivel up into Jesuology, and without the man Jesus there simply is no Christology.

The question is always about 'this man Jesus and more'. Jesus is more than a man full of grace, more than one of the great figures of mankind. He is not merely one of the many prophets who appeared in the course of mankind's history. In him there happened something decisive, something originating in God himself. From the early days of Christianity this was expressed when Christians confessed that in Jesus God gave us his only Son, somebody who was part of God's own 'self'. This sonship throws light on the ultimate depths of Jesus as such. Chalcedon, too, bore witness to this in its formula of 'one person in two natures'.

The original significance of a dogmatic statement is likely to get obscured in the course of history. Then it becomes inevitable that we ask ourselves what Chalcedon really meant to say. If we find the answer, the next question is naturally: Can we still express this in exactly the same terms? If Chalcedon found some kind of solution in the formula of 'one person in two natures', do these terms still mean the same thing to us? Catechetical and pastoral experience seem to tell us that this is definitely not the case.

Already at Chalcedon a number of bishops recoiled from the dogmatic character of the statement. Now, does this not show that there is a certain tension in the relations between teaching and preaching? Or between intellectual considerations and the life of faith? No amount of abstract doctrine can turn us into Christians: this depends on our concrete answer to the call embodied in Jesus. Christianity cannot be reduced to a doctrine. The real point is what Jesus means to us for our actual practical life. The preaching must affect our daily behaviour.

If a particular formulation of the message no longer appeals and has lost its effectiveness, we should have the courage to find another way of formulating the message. Obviously, even today we can only do this with exactly the same fumbling as happened in the past because we are no more able than our ancestors to find a definitive formula for the ineffable.

The letter of a dogmatic definition does not quite coincide with the truth it is meant to express. In other words: the truth aimed at always exceeds the limits of human concepts, and certainly the words to express them. One might say that Chalcedon was 'a' truth which may pave the way for 'the' truth. Because of this it seems more sensible to talk about the *in*tent of Chalcedon than about its actual *con*tent. The reason is that it is difficult to distinguish between content and concept. It is truly problematic whether one could convey exactly the same message with different concepts. There is no way of translating Chalcedon 'as such'. Other concepts are bound to have a different content or value. But the basic *intent* of a conciliar statement can indeed be respected by the use of different concepts.

Let us take the concept of human nature. Today people see this mainly as representing the human condition in its actual reality, and this condition is a matter of living and therefore constantly evolving. But it is precisely this sense of the dynamics of history, of the human condition as it is enacted in history, which was absent from, if not alien to, Chalcedon. What Chalcedon never envisaged was that the incarnation of the divine Logos presumes a kind of 'becoming' in God.

When the person or hypostasis of the Son of God becomes man, then he becomes a 'humanised' person, and today people find it impossible to see Jesus otherwise than as a person in the modern sense. An increasing number of theologians today are inclined to accept that the thesis, 'Jesus is *also* a human person' in the modern sense, is not in contradiction with Chalcedon.

Christ's human personality cannot be separated from his divine personality because the Son of God as a person became truly human. Today it is no longer possible to talk about Jesus as not being a human person. This would be the same as saying that he is not really a fully true human being, but this was not what Chalcedon wanted to say.

Today the personality value of man is understood as a way of defining the human being as such. Popular expressions, such as 'being treated as a person', 'to have personal relations with', 'personal growth and freedom' throw up an actual, cultural preoccupation, which one cannot just write off.

If we want to pursue the indications given by Chalcedon, we shall have to put Jesus right among ourselves with a human face that is personally recognisable and in which each of us can see himself. But at the same time we must confess him as the one Son of God in whom God shares our human condition in a way which cannot be done again.

Translated by T. L. Westow

Bibliography

de Halleux, A. 'La Définition christologique à Chalcédoine' *Revue Théologique de Louvain* 7 (1976) 3-23 and 155-170.
Grillmeier, A. *Jesus der Christus im Glauben der Kirche* I (Freiburg 1979).
Ibid. Christ in Christian Tradition I (London ²1975).
Ibid. Mit ihm und in ihm (Freiburg 1975).
Šagi-Busić, Th. '*Deus perfectus et homo perfectus*' *a Concilio Ephesino ad Chalcedonenese* (Rome 1965).

Studer, B. 'Consubstantialis Patri—consubstantialis matri: une antithèse christologique chez Léon le Grand' *Revue des Études Augustiniennes* 18 (1972) 87-115.

Smulders, P. 'Dogmengeschichtliche und lehramtliche Entfaltung der Christologie' *Mysterium Salutis* III/1 (Einsiedeln 1970) 389-476.

Maas, W. *Unveränderlichkeit Gottes* (Munich 1974).

van Beeck, F. J. *Christ proclaimed: Christology as rhetoric* (New York 1979).

Sesboüé, B. 'Le Procès contemporain de Chalcédoine' *Recherches de Science Religieuse* 65 (1977) 45-79.

PART III

What sense can the use of the term 'Son of God' have in Non-Christian cultures, such as that of Asia?

Aloysius Pieris

Speaking of the Son of God in Non-Christian Cultures, e.g., in Asia

1. THE TWO CHRISTOLOGICAL PERSPECTIVES IN ASIA TODAY

(a) The Focus on Religions

ANY CHRISTOLOGICAL inquiry into the Asian cultures will stumble against the fact that neither Jesus nor the religion he founded has won large-scale acceptance in Asia. Gotama, the Buddha, and Muhammad, the Prophet, are household names in the East, but Jesus the Christ is hardly invoked by the vast majority (over 97 per cent) of our people. Yet, Jesus was no less an Asian than the founders of Buddhism and Islam. Even of the few who believe in him, how many recall that God's Word had chosen to become Asian in wanting to be human? And how is it that the first Asians who heard him on our behalf and gave us the normative interpretations of his divine sonship, made a significant breakthrough in the West but failed to penetrate the complex cultural ethos of Asia?

Asia's later disillusion with the 'Colonial Christ', no doubt, added to this estrangement. But it also revealed that Christ could make sense in our cultures only to the extent that we use the soteriological idiom of 'non-Christian' religions. We infer this from the fact that, when Jesus re-entered the continent of his birth as the white colonizer's tribal god seeking ascendancy in the Asian pantheon, it was often the non-Christian religions that awakened the cultural ego of subdued nations in their collision with Christian powers, so that after four centuries of colonialism, Asia would lose only about 2 per cent of her population to Christianity! If the Philippines succumbed to Christendom it was because no other major Asian religion had struck institutional roots there earlier. The rapid rate of Christianisation in South America, contemporary Africa and Oceania, in contrast with Asia's persistent defiance of the Christian kerygma, confirms our thesis: *that the door which was once closed to Jesus in Asia is the only door that can take him in today, namely, the soteriological nucleus or the liberative core of various religions that have given shape and stability to our cultures*.

We stress the words *soteriological* and *liberative*, for, there is also a *sinful* and *enslaving* dimension to Asian religiosity. In a theological discourse such as this, therefore, one must discern the authentic core of an Asian religion from its perverted forms. It is the former that provides the indigenous idiom for a meaningful Christ-talk in Asia. The failure to perceive this distinction accounts for the two Christological perspectives prevailing today in the Asian church: a *Christ-against-religions* theology (of western inspiration) and a *Christ-of-religions* theology, which have emerged dialectically in three successive versions.

The Christ-*against*-religions theology appeared in its crudest version when the colonial Christ came to redeem Asia's pagan soul from the grip of superstition through the medium of a western culture. Even De Nobili, Ricci and others offered only a minor emendation to this 'Christology' in that they used the 'pagan' culture itself as their medium to draw the Asians from their religions to that of Christ. But India's three-century search for the non-colonial Christ[1] with Hindu participation too (see below) culminated with what is called 'Indian Christology'—actually, a misnomer for a Christ-*of*-religions theology concerned with Hinduism[2]—which anticipated the fulfilment theory of the Lambeth Conference of 1930 and the Vatican Council of 1962: Christ works in all religions as the final consummation of all human search for redemption.

This theory, however, has already boomeranged on the Asian church. From the Buddhists she hears that Jesus is only *a* 'bodhisattva' (aspirant for Enlightenment) while Gotama is *the* Buddha; from the Muslims, that he is *a* prophet albeit a special one, while Muhammad remains *the* prophet. Thus her own assertion that Jesus is *the* Son, *the* Christ, *the* Lord before whom other religious founders are mere prophets and precursors, is just one rival claim among others! Even Rahner's 'anonymous Christianity' has been anticipated in Hinduism which tends to gather other religions under its own salvific umbrella neutralising their uniqueness. According to a recent version of it, all religions are 'alternate absolutes' with one undivided Goal, like the radii of a circle having but one centre.[3] Hinduism, for the average Hindu, cannot but be the whole circle though a Christian may hope to prove that Christ is its centre! Buddhists have similarly appealed to their belief in the 'solitary buddhas' (*Pacceka buddha*) to postulate the possibility of a non-Buddhist attaining Nirvana outside institutional Buddhism but never outside the truth that the Buddha has discovered.[4]

(b) The Contextual Approach

The fulfilment theory failed also in that it ignored the discomforting issue of *poverty* which is as much a component of the Asian context as religiosity. Besides, is not the story of Jesus pre-eminently the story of God-*with*-the-poor, God-*of*-the-poor and God-*for*-the-poor? When the problem was reviewed, especially in the Sixties, the two Christological perspectives were again in evidence. The neo-colonialist school held that non-Christian religions were a positive hindrance to the humanising task of eradicating poverty in Asia, a task which only Christianity, with its own (western) model of 'development', could achieve.[5] I even recall it being described as 'pre-evangelisation', a prelude to Christ's arrival on the scene!

But a counter-thesis was offered by the Christian ashrams where a contemplative adventure with God-in-Jesus was made to mirror Asia's own *religious* perception of *poverty*. According to the eastern ascesis of detachment, *opted* poverty would be the redemptive antidote to acquisitiveness which is the sin that generates *enforced* poverty. By giving a community-orientation to those liberative values of Asian religiosity and poverty through common life and solidarity with the poor around, the Christian ashram matured into a living Christological formula through which Jesus was commemorated as 'God-become-poor' and celebrated as the 'divine guru' who offers interior liberation from greed, and gathers the *religious poor* around himself into a saved and saving peoplehood: a replica of an inculturated church.

But, was this ashramic Christ concerned about the colossal scandal of organised greed thriving on religious sanction? What about the sinful dimension of religiosity and poverty? Do inculturationists believe that voluntary poverty, when leavened by the liberative essence of Asian religiosity, could serve as a *prophetic* posture and a *political* strategy against enforced poverty, as it did in Gandhi's own case? We sympathise, therefore, with the Asian liberation theologians' insistence that *God-Man* Jesus saves by being at once the *human* victim and the *divine* judge of Asia's institutionalised misery (Matt. 25:31 ff.). They demand that authentic Christianity, which embodies this revolutionary activity of God's Son, be made to contest its own enslaving institutionalism. But they hardly grant that Asian religions, too, have such prophetico-political resources which a Christian minority must appropriate. The encounter with Christ which they rightly see in Asia's struggle for full humanity, implies for them, therefore, a rejection of Asian religiosity *in toto*. Theirs is a Christ-*against*-religions theology which carries its colonialist and neo-colonialist versions of the past into a crypto-colonialist finale; for it replaces 'culture' and 'development' of the previous eras with structural 'liberation' which is imported into Asia without first allowing Asia to liberate it of its restrictive notion of 'religion', a notion derived from three non-Asian sources: (*a*) Latin American liberationists' early unilateral rejection of religion as a human alienation—based, in turn, on (*b*) an unrevised nineteenth-century Marxian analysis of religions, and (*c*) western biblical (e.g., Barthian) interpretation of religion(s) as anti-thetical to faith.

This conflict between the inculturationists' Christ-*of*-religions theology and the liberationists' Christ-*against*-religions theology erupted even as late as 1979 at the Third World Theologians' Asian Consultation.[6] When we proposed the 'religiosity-poverty' polarity as the context of Asian theology,[7] some theologians too hastily reduced religiosity to 'inculturation' and poverty to 'liberation'! Hence we repeat the plea we made during the subsequent controversy[8] to abandon the inculturation-liberation debate, since religiosity and poverty in their coalescence provide both the *cultural* context and the *liberationist* thrust required in any Asian Christology. Besides, are they not the two perspectives along which Jesus Himself revealed his divine sonship to his first Asian followers?

2. TWO PERSPECTIVES FOR A CHRISTOLOGY IN ASIA TODAY

(*b*) Return to Jesus

Missiologists in the West have been disturbed by the recent news that some Asian theologians refuse to admit the 'uniqueness of Christ'. Not only 'Christ' but even the word 'Christology' are used here purely as conventional terms indispensable in an inter-ecclesial theological discourse. But the fact is that 'Christ' (like 'Son of God' or 'Lord') is only a title, a human categorisation by which one particular culture tried to 'capture' the ineffable mystery of salvation communicated in the person and teaching of Jesus. What is absolute and unique is not the title, but what all major religions, some in theistic, others in non-theistic terms, have professed for centuries as the mystery of salvation manifesting itself at least in a trinal (if not trinitarian) form:

(1) Salvation as the *salvific 'beyond'* becoming the human person's *salvific 'within'* (e.g., Yahweh, Allah, Tao, Nirvana, Tathatā, Brahman-Atman),

(2) thanks to a *salvific mediation* which is also revelatory in character (e.g., Tao, Marga, Dharma, Dabar, Image),

(3) and a (given) human *capacity for salvation* and/or a *saving power* paradoxically inherent in the human person (purusa, citta, ātman, etc.) despite his/her being sheer 'nothing', mere 'dust', 'soul-less' (anātma), a part of created 'illusion' (māyā) immersed in this cosmic 'vale of tears' (samsāra) from which one yearns for perfect redemption.

Whether we should name this (God-Logos-Pneuma; Father-Son-Spirit) or not name it at all, is not our immediate concern, but that this 'triune' mystery constitutes the basic soteriological datum in many of our religious cultures; that the significance of speaking of the 'Son of God' in such a context depends on the discovery of the *sensitive spot in the Asian heart*, where Jesus, by making us retell his story, would find the proper idiom to communicate his unique identity within that tridimensional mystery; and that this sensitive spot can be discovered by retracing the steps which Jesus himself had taken in his effort to reveal his person in the Asian context of religiosity and poverty.

We know clearly that Jesus evolved his self-understanding and his self-revelation by his 'baptismal immersion' into the Asian reality. Let us concentrate on the two representative moments of this immersion: his first prophetic gesture at Jordan and his last prophetic gesture on Calvary . . . both of which are designated in the gospels as 'baptism'.[9] Jesus' self-effacing gesture at the Jordan insinuates a prior discernment as to what was enslaving and what was liberative in the religiosity of Israel. The narrow ideology of the Zealots, the sectarian puritanism of the Essenes, the self-righteous legalism of the Pharisees and the leisure-class mentality of the Sadducees had not impressed him. For he opted for the *politically dangerous* brand of *prophetic asceticism* practised by John the Baptiser. It was when he stepped into the Jordan to identify himself with the religious poor of the countryside and sought initiation under this great Asian guru, that he manifested his own salvific role to the people: the Lamb/Servant of God, the beloved Son (of God), the Word to be heard, the Giver of the Spirit . . . as the culture of the day phrased it. It was by entering into the soteriological nucleus of his culture that he revealed his salvific mission.

But Jordan was only the beginning of Calvary. The first baptism would soon lead to the other. Can there be an authentic religiosity without a painful participation in the conflicts of poverty? An Abba-experience without a struggle against Mammon? In fact the money-polluted religiosity of his day conspired with the foreign colonial power—the inveterate alliance between religion and Mammon persisting to this day in Asia—to plant the cross where alone he could reveal his true identity: Truly this was the Son of God (Mark 15:39).

One thing is certain. If the revelatory and mediational dimension of the salvation-mystery (which has never ceased to shine like an unsetting sun on the soteriological horizon of Asia) should manifest itself unambiguously in the human event of Jesus, then that event is pre-eminently the trajectory which, *today*, links the Jordan of Asian religiosity with the Calvary of Asian poverty. It is there that the Asian cultures will open their repertoire of titles, symbols and formulas to express their new discovery; then the Asian church will sing not one but a thousand new canticles to her Spouse and Lord.

(b) The New Asian Formula

The first meaningful Christological formula—one that would be at once homologous and kerygmatic, i.e., one that would make sense to Christians and non-Christians alike, is an authentically Asian church, which obviously is a far cry from the esoteric community that she is today, ranting as she does in the occult language of the colonial founders to be understood only by the initiated. To pull herself out of this *incommunicado* situation, she must be given time to step into the baptismal waters of Asian religiosity and to pass through the passion and death on the cross of Asian poverty. Until this *ecclesiological revolution* is complete, there will be no Asian Christology. Instead, we shall have to be satisfied with mere 'Christological reflections' focused either on the problem of the 'poor' (Kappan, Balasuriya, etc.) or on 'religions' (Kadowaki, Abhishiktananda); or, as in the case of the extensive Indian hermeneusis of the fourth gospel,[10] we shall rest content with the 'political' standpoints and the 'mystical' viewpoints of our theologians. But these can only be the stirrings of a more radical desire to see Jesus' integral approach to asceticism and politics, to religions and the poor, educing Christologies from the soteriological depths of our cultures.

Such a possibility is not remote. For the desired *ecclesiological revolution* has already begun in the fringes of the Church, where little laboratories of hope (for the moment few and far between) are struggling to be born. If they are in the periphery of the mainline churches, it is because they have moved to the very centre of Asian reality. Their ambition to fuse politics with asceticism, involvement with introspection, class-analysis with self-analysis, the Marxist *laborare* with the monastic *orare*, a militant repudiation of Mammon with a mystical relationship with Abba their Father . . . has plunged them into the liberative streams of both religiosity and poverty. We hope that their *participation* ('baptismal immersion') in the twofold Asian reality would soon bloom into a spontaneous *explicitation* ('Christic apocalypse') of the many hidden theologies issuing out of the soteriological premises of Asian religions. That is how Christologies would be born in our continent. It is the story of Jesus retold by those Asian Christians who have dared to traverse Jesus' own path from Jordan to Calvary.

Unquestionably this *participation-explicitation* approach to Asian Christology ought to be complemented by a parallel search for that sensitive zone in the Asian soul where Asia's own characteristic response to Jesus will be disclosed. Our suggestion is that non-Christian sages be encouraged to tell *their own* story of Jesus. We are not referring to intellectuals and their 'theory of religions' which we have dismissed in the earlier part of our inquiry. We speak rather of those *religious* seekers who have opted to be *poor* in their search for the Saving Truth and would, during their pilgrimage, encounter Jesus within their own soteriological perspectives.

This is not a dream, but a reality with a century and a half of history behind it. From about 1820, many convinced Hindus have been grappling with the mystery of Jesus. Whatever be one's reaction to their gnostic interpretations, in them one can sense how Jesus makes his entry into a given Asian ethos. Some of these Hindus might have acknowledged Jesus as Saviour (e.g., Subha Rao) while many 'followed Him from a distance' like Peter (e.g., Raj Ram Mohan Roy, Kesham Chandra, etc.).[11] Even trinitarian speculations were not absent in their 'Christologies'. But the fact that their interest in Jesus grew during the Hindu renaissance deserves attention. As the Hindu self-consciousness was awakened by the challenge of a politically extravagant western Christianity, *some* of these pilgrims of truth might have found in Jesus 'the socio-political texture of sanctity' they were looking for. The aim of their search perhaps was not an 'ontological union' of God and Man in the one person of Jesus, but the 'moral imperative' of reconciling *God-experience* with *human concern* in one identical salvific process. One understands why Gandhi looked upon Jesus as a model *Satyagrāhin*: 'the suffering servant of Truth', if I may coin a 'Christological title' that would describe the Gandhian Christ. Truth (God) triumphs through suffering endured by Jesus. The Hindu doctrine of renunciation allows the cross to shine as the supreme locus of Jesus' revelation of the divine. What was a scandal to the Jews and folly to the Greeks, could be wisdom to a Hindu! Since in today's Asia, both interior freedom of the soul and the structural emancipation of the socio-political order (now ideologically polarised) demand a meaningful paradigm of *renunciation* (opted poverty) to justify the human struggle for total human liberation in terms of a salvific encounter with the Ultimate Reality, one might legitimately ask whether Jesus' exaltation on the cross would not be that paradigm.

There are, of course, other 'sensitive spots' in other areas wherein Jesus may find access to the Asian ethos under other names and titles, through other parables and paradigms. Our surmise, therefore, is that a meaningful discourse on the 'Son of God' will come about in our cultures mainly through an in-depth dialogue between *those* peripheral Christian communities and *these* non-Christian disciples of Christ trying to re-tell the story of Jesus to one another in terms of that one absolute triune mystery of salvation.

Notes

1. For a list of the relevant writings from 1600 to 1965, see K. Baago *Library of Indian Christian Theology, A Bibliography* (Madras 1969).

2. For a summary, see R. H. S. Boyd *An Introduction to Indian Christian Theology* (Madras 1969); K. Baago *Pioneers of Indigenous Christianity* (Bangalore 1969).

3. K. Sivaraman 'Resources in Hindu Morality and Religion' *Towards World Community: the Colombo Papers* ed. S. J. Samartha (Geneva 1975) p. 28.

4. K. N. Jayatilleke *The Buddhist Attitude to Other Religions* (Ceylon 1966) p. 16.

5. The most articulate exposition of this thesis in the Sixties was A. Th. Van Leeuwen *Christianity in World History: the Meeting of Faiths of East and West* (London 1964). But the theory was being circulated even in the Seventies, e.g., P. Gheddo *Why is the Third World Poor?* (New York 1973) pp. 30-37 and *passim*.

6. See the relevant documents in *Asia's Struggle for Full Humanity* ed. V. Fabella (New York 1980).

7. *Ibid.* pp. 75-95.

8. See *Voices from the Third World* 2, No. 1 (June 1979).

9. Matt. 3:13-17 and parallels; Mark 10:38, 39; Luke 12:50. For a theological excursus on this theme, see my 'The Mission of the Local Church and the Major Religious Traditions' a paper read at *The Sedes Seminar* (March 1981, Rome), now in the press (New York).

10. See M. R. Spindler 'Recent Indian Studies of the Gospel of John: Puzzling Contextualisation' *Exchange* 9 No. 27 (December 1980) 1-56.

11. For an excellent study of these 'Christologies', see M. M. Thomas *The Acknowledged Christ of Indian Renaissance* (London 1969), and S. J. Samartha *Hindus vor dem Universalen Christus, Beiträge zu einer Christologie Indien* (Stuttgart 1970).

PART IV

*Towards a Synthesis: A Reflection on the Issue as a
Whole*

F

Karl Rahner

Christology Today
(Instead of a Conclusion)

THE EDITORS of this volume, J-B. Metz and E. Schillebeeckx, have pressed me to write some sort of conclusion to the volume. I do not know how to satisfy their wish. The current debates in Christology have scarcely reached a stage at which final conclusions can be drawn, if indeed such a thing is possible at all. It certainly is not possible in a couple of pages at the end of a slim volume. And then I really do not know whether I have anything to say about Christology that I have not said long ago. So how am I to satisfy my friends' wish? I am not going to pass judgment on this volume. I shall just say a couple of things which come more from my heart than my rational intellect.

I

First, I believe that even today a Catholic theologian should not simply ignore the classical formulations of Catholic theology. It is true that a dogma and its formulation in tradition and the *magisterium* of the Church are not simply the same, but at least in the cases of Christology the traditional formulation is not so easily superseded that we are now in a position to dispense with it. We do not come so easily by formulations of our own that on the level of preaching or of the expression of our individual faith we have no more use for the old formulation. We cannot treat it as no more than a statement which belongs wholly to the earlier history of the interpretation of faith, even though it may as such of course still be normative for the serious theologian.

We theologians of today have to be cool and self-critical about ourselves. We must not just be people who think they have learnt things from the history of the faith, but people who are still willing to learn from it! If we were willing in this way, how could we be prepared simply to abandon the old Christological formulations in favour of our own reformulations? Even if we grant that it might in the future be justified, because of historical transformations in language, to express the reality embodied in Christology in a totally different way (totally different only in preaching), by the strict criteria of the sociology of ideas this future has certainly not come yet. A person may of course feel that it is his or her duty as a theologian to explore this future on behalf of the Church, but such a person must take care that he or she does not lose contact with the mass of the

73

faithful behind them, including the bishops. This concern is another essential part of a genuinely Catholic theology, even if the pace of the march into the future of the faith seems rather slow to the impatient.

On the other hand it is equally important to see that even the most sacred and permanent formulations of the faith need explaining, in other words that they inevitably have to be expanded by the addition of other statements, albeit differing widely in their normative status. (John Paul II insists on the word 'transubstantiation' in the doctrine of the Eucharist. I as a poor theologian must ask questions and say what is really meant by the phrase 'substance of the bread' and 'transformation of substance' here, because they can be taken to mean many things which are not correct and rightly seem meaningless to a modern physicist.) In explaining the binding tenets of dogma, therefore, one must not imagine that such statements are simple and clear or could not mislead. However, if in the process one thinks not just a little but explores all the implications to the best of one's powers, then the old formulations themselves, and obedience to them, lead in certain circumstances to statements in Christology which will surprise many who have listened to the old formulae in peaceful familiarity and thought they understood what they were saying. (The dogma of the true humanity of Jesus, for example, as it has always been proclaimed, gives rise to insights about the historical shaping of Jesus' consciousness and about the possibility that his consciousness might even undergo religious development. In the past these insights were ignored or even denied by the expounders of this dogma.)

So one approach (not the only one) of a Catholic dogmatic theologian ought to be to use the old Christological formulations to obtain the new insights which seem important and indispensable if his present-day Christology is to have a positive relationship to present ways of thinking (including critical exegesis and the rest). It is one way in which he can arrive at new formulations and they do not have to eliminate the old ones, nor do they have to be obtained through a merely negative criticism or overthrowing of the classical formulations of Christology. The results of such a co-existence between old and (quite necessary and legitimate) new formulations on the everyday awareness of faith in the Church, and the eventual balance between old and new in the ordinary Christian's religious consciousness and in the Church's official proclamation, all this naturally cannot be programmed in advance and can safely be left to the future history of the faith. It is, however, obvious that even in Christology history is not at an end and that true orthodoxy does not consist in a mere (desperate and stubborn) repetition of the old Christological formulations which grew up in history and will continue to be part of that history. But their place in history is also the very reason why we cannot pass them over in silence as though they had no force for us any more. An exegete should do his exegesis and biblical theology and, as an exegete, no more, but I have no time for a Catholic exegete who shows no sign of ever having heard of the Council of Chalcedon. One must carry the past with one in an authentic way if one is to win a future for Christology. Rome must honestly watch over the purity of Christology and stress the normative character of the Church's old official Christology, but if this were to be done in such a way that it left no room for recognition of the need for new formulations of Christology, it would be a betrayal of the task of proclamation tomorrow.

I may accept the words of the Johannine prologue with a faith so firm I am ready to die for it. I may allow them force and life as one of the foundations of my own theology. I may firmly and cheerfully let myself be overwhelmed by the bright darkness of God's revelation and refuse to be a clever rationalist, but even so I am allowed to tremble at the bottom of my heart and spirit when I read, 'And the word was made flesh', and I may wonder what it in fact means and what it does not mean. I have the right to ask the question if at the same time I think of the incomprehensibility and immeasurability of the God of a vast cosmos, and if I also maintain in faith that this God is and remains unchangeable in himself, that he is indescribably greater than anything that is or can be imagined outside him (and so than Jesus' created being). Jesus' human soul, I must believe, as a human soul, contemplates what is for it, too, the enduring incomprehensibility of God in adoration from an infinite distance of creatureliness. Despite all this it remains true that the word was made flesh.

But I refuse, as I consider this article of faith, to forget the other articles of faith to make things easier for me. For that reason we must constantly ask what Christology is really trying to say and what it is not trying to say, even if classical Christology must constantly be one of the starting-points for this inquiry. The recent offerings in present-day Christology in all the churches are not necessarily always happy in their new formulations, but we should examine them with respect and love and not imagine ourselves superior to them in an orthodoxy which would ultimately remain sterile. When a little while ago a professor in Rome began his lecture with the statement that Schillebeeckx's Christology was heretical and therefore he would not talk about it, such a Christology is condemning itself out of its own mouth to be ignored by people of today and to be no more than the internal ideology of a steadily diminishing group.

II

Any present-day Christology must be a 'Christology of ascent'. The name does not matter, but a Catholic theology which holds fast to the necessity and importance of fundamental theology, which takes history seriously as the locus of revelation, which cannot survive today without bringing about a more intense interaction between fundamental theology and dogmatics, such a theology must start from the real, historical Jesus of Nazareth. When one starts from here, the reports in the story of Jesus cannot be read first of all as dogmatic propositions, made into a revelation by inspiration. In the ordinary empirical development of theology faith in Jesus precedes convictions about the Church and its *magisterium* and the inspiration of the New Testament. There is no need to deny a degree of reciprocal influence among all the elements of the Christian faith, but in the end this makes no difference to the fact that Jesus is the source of belief in the Church and Scripture and not, ultimately, vice-versa. In such a Christology of ascent it is perfectly proper for statements about the significance of Jesus 'for us' (which of course express a reality 'in itself') to be made first because statements about something existing purely 'in itself', whose significance for us is explained only subsequently will not be listened to, at least not by people today, and are not appropriate. The *propter nos* of the Credo can be quite happily said at the beginning. When this is done in the right way, it turns out that what seems to be supremely anthropocentric refers to a man who only finds himself by letting go and surrendering to the incomprehensibility of God. First in Christology comes the question, 'What does he mean for us?', and then the question 'Who must he be if he has this significance for us?'

Of course this significance can be described in a great variety of ways, and naturally the arguments in support will need to be similarly various. All, however, must start from the encounter with the historical Jesus and with the courage (itself shown 'transcendentally' to be legitimate and necessary) to endure all the unavoidable difficulties involved in the origin of an absolute choice in a historical reality. All such demonstrations of the absolute significance of Jesus for us, because they are always and inevitably finite, will in their detailed argument, make one point clear, express another only vaguely and perhaps ignore and forget a third. The particular outlines of these arguments will vary, with people, cultures and periods. It would not be praiseworthy, but problematic and alarming, if these arguments in the Church were too uniform.

III

With the caveat about the absolute validity of this necessary plurality of approaches to and aspects of the significance of Jesus for us, I will venture to say that these approaches and aspects (they are the same thing) inevitably mean *two fundamental insights*. Whether an emphasis on them is supposed to characterise 'my' Christology or any orthodox Christology is in the end of no interest to me.

(*a*) First, I have to see Jesus, through his reality and his word, as the unsurpassable access to the immediacy of God in himself, not just as an access to this immediacy as idea and possibility, but as the inherently victorious promise of the realisation of that immediacy. I shall try to make this a bit clearer, leaving open the question whether the required constituents of an absolute religion are to be found only in him or whether the idea is intelligible independently and only its realisation has to be recognised through and in Jesus.

Absolute and fundamentally unsurpassable intimacy with God, such as is perfected in the beatific vision, is the precondition for the genuine universality of a religion. Without this a religion can only be regional, particular, popular, culture-specific, etc., inevitably, because it can know only a finite message of salvation, alongside which, by definition, others must exist. This closeness, if it is to commit God in himself, can only be understood as grace deriving from God's loving freedom. This grace can be thought of either in the form of a more or less neutral offer to human freedom or in the form of the actual God-given victory of the offer, establishing itself by its own power in and through human freedom. There is naturally also—in theory—another form, absolute rejection by human beings, resulting in the final catastrophe of human history.

In Jesus (and ultimately only in him) we learn, through his life and work, that the history of the offer of an absolute self-communication of God to the human race has entered a new phase. In this phase (rightly called both the final phase in the history of human freedom and its first real beginning) the victory of God's offer of himself to the human race has become irrevocable, as a result of God's action and not merely *a posteriori* as a result of actual free human choices. Jesus is God's promise of himself to the human race, essentially absolutely unlimited and existentially now in a stage of eschatological irrevocability.

My task here is not to verify this interpretation of Jesus historically. It is, however, implicit in Jesus' proclamation that the kingdom of God has come in him, his message and his work, when one realises that the kingdom of God, if it is to be really definitive and more than an earthly kingdom, must be identical with God in himself and must burst the bounds of a model in which God relates to the world only as the creator and preserver of a world different from him, with its own possibilities and goals. With the obvious proviso that saving history is such that another way in which it is a reality is through word and as a word which occurs as a reality, I venture to say: *the statement that Jesus is the irreversible self-pledging of the God who communicates himself, and not a reality created by him, as the content and goal of history, is inevitably coterminous with classical christology's statement about the 'hypostatic union'*. I shall not go into this further here. Suffice it to say that if these statements are really coterminous (and I am convinced that they are), it is possible to make an 'orthodox' Christological statement which both inherently implies a 'Christology for us' and also stands alongside the classical formulation of Christology and so performs a critical function in relation to possible misunderstandings of classical Christology (especially Monophysite views, which are still strong today). Of course the same critical function is also performed in the opposite direction, by classical Christology on the newly proposed formulation.

(*b*) There is one point at which I must clarify and elaborate what I have just said. If Jesus is to be God's victorious self-pledging in history, the historical fact of this victory and its manifestation is only conceivable if it is seen as the irrevocable *acceptance* of this divine offer in Jesus. This definitive and irrevocable acceptance of God's pledging of himself, visible in history, can be conceived as taking place only through what we call, in Christian language, Jesus' death and resurrection. A theology of freedom could show that, however many ways there may be of interpreting the specific response of freedom to its determination by death, death, and only death, is the event by which freedom's choice becomes final. Even though the particular form of Jesus' death may be an essential element of saving history, the underlying importance of Jesus' death to saving history is that it makes final the acceptance of God's offer of himself to Jesus (and in him to the human race). Naturally either here or at another point in our discussion there should ideally be an explanation of why and how there exists an unbreakable solidarity between Jesus and his fate and the human race, such that God's pledging of himself to him and his acceptance of this promise through him in his death is really God's promise of himself to the human race as a whole. But there is no room for that here.

What I have been saying amounts to no more than a few isolated and inadequate suggestions about the sort of Christology required today. One could go on for ever. It would do no harm for a present-day Christology to elaborate the ideas of someone like Teilhard de Chardin with more precision and clarity, even though in his work it is not always that clear what intelligible and orthodox connection exists between Jesus of Nazareth and the cosmic Christ, the Omega Point of world evolution.

Above all, however, such a Christology for today and tomorrow would have to say much more than in the past about the totally personal loving relationship of the individual human being to Jesus of Nazareth. This could perhaps be described very simply and yet radically in such a way that the whole of classical Christology would in fact be included in it and this classical Christology would lose the off-putting appearance it often has today even for firmly believing Christians. If this relationship of the individual to Jesus were from the outset clearly understood as *a dying with Jesus (in absolute hope) in a surrender to the incomprehensibility of the eternal God*, Christology would no longer appear to the other world religions and the other forms of human desire for God as compatible only with a particular religion, which cannot be that of all human beings.

Translated by Francis McDonagh

Contributors

TARSICIUS J. VAN BAVEL, OSA, was born in 1923 in Tilburg (Holland), and became a member of the Augustinian Friars. After obtaining his degree in Fribourg (Switzerland), where he specialised in patrology, he lectured in theology in various institutes in Belgium and Holland. In 1969 he was appointed ordinary professor at the Catholic University of Louvain in charge of christology and patrology, a position he has held ever since. He is also director of the Augustinian Historical Institute at Heverlee (Belgium). Among his publications are: *Recherches sur la christologie de saint Augustin* (1954); *Christians in the world: Introduction to the spirituality of St Augustine* (1980—the original was published in Dutch in 1970).

HERBERT HAAG was born in 1915. He read philosophy, theology and oriental studies in Rome, Paris, Fribourg (Switzerland), Leyden and Boston, gaining a doctorate in theology in Fribourg in 1942. Ordained priest in 1940, he was engaged in parish work from 1942-48. He became a member of the Pontifical Biblical Commission in 1947. He was professor for Old Testament in Lucerne (1948-60) and Tübingen (1960-80), and retired in 1980. His most important publications are *Bibel-Lexikon* (ed.) (2nd ed. 1968); *Biblische Schöpfungslehre und kirchliche Erbsündenlehre* (4th ed. 1968); *Abschied vom Teufel* (6th ed. 1978); *Vom alten zum neuen Pascha. Geschichte und Theologie des Osterfestes* (1971); *Teufelsglaube* (2nd ed. 1979); *Und du sollst fröhlich sein. Lebensbejahung im Alten Testament* (1978); *Das Land der Bibel* (2nd ed. 1978); *Vor dem Bösen ratlos?* (1978); *Du hast mich verzaubert. Liebe und Sexualität in der Bibel* (1980); *Der Fall Küng* (with N. Greinacher) (1980); *Das Buch des Bundes. Augsätze zur Bibel und ihrer Umwelt* (1980).

BAS VAN IERSEL, SMM, was born in 1924 at Heerlen, Holland; he joined the de Montfort Fathers and was ordained a priest in 1950. He studied at the universities of Nijmegen and Louvain, is a doctor of theology and professor of exegesis of the New Testament at the University of Nijmegen; he is also a co-editor of *Tijdschrift voor Theologie* and of the review *Schrift*. Of his published works we mention: *'Der Sohn' in den synoptischen Jesusworten* (1961).

NICHOLAS LASH was born in India in 1934. A Roman Catholic, he has been, since 1978, Norris-Hulse professor of divinity in the University of Cambridge. His publications include: *His Presence in the World* (1968); *Change in Focus* (1973); *Newman on Development* (1975); *Voices of Authority* (1976); *Theology on Dover Beach* (1979); and *A Matter of Hope: A Theologian's Reflections on the Thought of Karl Marx* (1981).

BRIAN McDERMOTT, SJ, was born in 1937 in New York City. Ordained in 1968, he received degrees from Fordham University, Woodstock College, Union Theological Seminary and the University of Nijmegen, where he acquired the doctorate. He is currently associate professor of systematic theology at Weston School of Theology, Cambridge, Massachusetts. He co-authored *Patterns of Promise, Christian Doctrine Yesterday, Today and Tomorrow* (1968) and is author of *The Personal Unity of Jesus and God according to Wolfhart Pannenberg* (1973) and articles in *Theological Studies, Chicago Studies* and *Spirituality Today*, among others.

ALOYSIUS PIERIS, SJ, was born in 1934 in Sri Lanka and is the founder-director of *TULANA*, a Buddhist-Christian Centre for research and encounter located in Kelaniya, a suburb of Colombo. A Classical Indologist specialised in Buddhology, he is at present engaged in a vast research project on medieval Pali (Buddhist) philosophical literature on which he has begun publishing a series of papers. Author of numerous articles on the 'contextualisation' of theology in Asia, he is also the co-editor of *Dialogue*, an international review for Buddhists and Christians published by the Ecumenical Institute of Colombo. He has been lecturing in several universities in Europe and USA (Gregorian, Rome, Graduate Theological Union, Berkeley, etc.) and is the professor of Asian Religions and Philosophies at the East Asian Pastoral Institute, Manila. As the theological consultant of the Christian Workers' Fellowship in Sri Lanka for the last thirteen years, he has been involved with the organisation of Buddhist-Marxist-Christian trialogues and encounters.

JON SOBRINO, SJ, a Basque by origin, was born in 1938. He has been a Jesuit since 1956, in the Latin American Province since 1957. He was ordained in 1969 and lives in El Salvador. He holds a degree in philosophy and a master's degree in engineering from the University of St Louis, and a doctorate in theology from Frankfurt. His major published works are *Christology at the Crossroads* (1978) and *La Resurrección de la verdadera Iglesia* (1981).

GEOFFREY WAINWRIGHT was born in 1939 in Yorkshire, England. He is a minister of the British Methodist Church. After studies in Cambridge, Geneva and Rome he became professor of systematic theology at the Protestant Faculty of Theology in Yaoundé, Cameroon (1967-73). Next he taught at The Queen's College, Birmingham, England. In 1979 he was called to Union Theological Seminary, New York, where he is now Roosevelt Professor of Systematic Theology. His books include *Christian Initiation* (1969); *Eucharist and Eschatology* (1971; [4]1981); and a systematic theology entitled *Doxology: The Praise of God in Worship, Doctrine and Life* (1980). He co-edited *The Study of Liturgy* (1978), is an editor of *Studia Liturgica* and an advisory editor of *One in Christ*. Dr Wainwright is a member of the Faith and Order Commission of the World Council of Churches.

DIETRICH WIEDERKEHR, OFMCap, born in 1933, is a Capuchin friar who is professor of fundamental theology at the theological faculty of Lucerne, Switzerland. He has written about Christology in *Mysterium Salutis* III:1 (1970) and in *Theologische Berichte* II and VII (1973 and 1978). He has published *Glaube an Erlösung. Konzepte der Soteriologie* (1976).

CONCILIUM